NATIONAL MINORITIES

Who Are They?

NATIONAL MINORITIES
Who Are They?

NICOLA GIRASOLI

1828

AKADÉMIAI KIADÓ, BUDAPEST

This book has been published with the support of the
INTER-EURÓPA BANK RT.—BUDAPEST

The author thanks for the co-operation
of Dr. Pier Franco Rubatto, Managing Director

ISBN 963 05 6866 7

Published by
Akadémiai Kiadó, H–1117 Budapest, Prielle Kornélia u. 19–35

Printed in Hungary
by Akadémiai Kiadó és Nyomda, Budapest

Preface

The issue of minorities is multifaceted and thus requires a multifaceted approach. Both at the national and international levels, lawyers, economists, diplomats and politicians, practicioners as well as scholars, governmental and non-governmental people can contribute to addressing and solving the many questions which are part and parcel of the complex issue of minorities. Their activities, insofar as they are aimed at a better understanding of the issues at hand and contribute to their resolution, should be welcomed.

It is my sincere wish that the present volume will also be granted a constructive role in the debate on minority issues. It takes the scholarly approach. Discussing the concept of minority and trying to establish the elements for a new definition, the author takes a wide view, encompassing centuries of history and a number of international organizations including the Conference on Security and Co-operation in Europe (recently rechristened Organization on Security and Co-operation in Europe). Touching upon many questions, some of which have not yet been definetively answered, his discourse will no doubt give rise to discussions. Apart from its scholarly merits, if it helps us to clarify our conceptual thinking in this regard it will certainly have served a useful purpose.

Max van der Stoel
OSCE High Commissioner on National Minorities

Contents

Abbreviations

ADDENDUM	General Comment Adopted by Human Rights Committee under Article 40, Paragraph 4, of the International Covenant on Civil and Political Rights—CCPR/C/21/Rev./1/Add.5—1994
CAHMIN	Committee for the Protection of National Minorities
CCPR	International Covenant on Civil and Political Rights (U.N. 1966)
CHD	Conference on the Human Dimension of the CSCE
CoEMIN	The Council of Europe and Minorities
CSCE	Conference on Security and Co-operation in Europe recently renamed: Organization on Security and Co-operation in Europe (OSCE)
CSO	Committee of Senior Officials
DECLARATION	Declaration on the Rights of Persons Belonging to National or Ethnic, Religious and Linguistic Minorities (U.N. 1992)
ECHR	European Convention on Human Rights and Fundamental Freedoms (Council of Europe 1950)
ECMM	European Community Monitoring Mission
HCNM	OSCE High Commissioner on National Minorities
NGO	Non-Governmental Organization
NNA States	Neutral and Non-Aligned States
ODIHR	Office for Democratic Institutions and Human Rights
P.C.I.J.	Permanent Court of International Justice
U.N.	United Nations Organization
UNESCO	United Nations Educational, Scientific and Cultural Organization

Introduction

Very often the concept of a "multicultural-society" considers many types of "cultural-pluralism" that are almost impossible to understand.

This can happen also because concepts like "multicultural" or "pluralism" are "mosaics" which consider all the different communities living in the same country: national minorities, ethnic groups, immigrants, foreign labour work force, refugees, the political asylum seekers. Viewed in this way most countries of the world could be called "multicultural".[1]

This confusion does not permit us to perceive the different social, cultural and political peculiarities of each of these groups. With reference to the pluralism by which these groups function, this way of thinking does not take into account the vast variety of problems faced by immigrants on the one hand, and national minorities on the other. Problems should be clearly identified and analysed in detail, in order to choose and adopt the right approach, and they should consider also the fact that in the future the idea of who is an immigrant and who is not, who belongs to a minority and who does not, will become more unclear.

[1] *See generally*: Perotti, A., Pluralismo culturale e minoranze—Ambiguità da evitare, in: *People on the Move*, XXII, March 1993, pp. 9–19

The aim of this book is to provide a better understanding of the concept of national minority. My intention is to try to eliminate some of the ambiguity generated by the erroneous presentation of the concept of a "multicultural society", which does not underline the diversity as well as the characteristics of the "real" communities. I would like also to highlight the differences that exist among the above-mentioned groups in relation to society in general.

A precise definition of national minority is not simple. International bodies like the U.N., CSCE and the Council of Europe have spent at least a decade at such an exercise without achieving success. Most of the international, regional and national documents on the protection of national minorities are excellent instruments for recognizing, respecting and promoting the specific identities of the individuals and groups of people who belong to national minorities, however, we rarely find a clear description of the very concept of national minorities.

Since the Helsinki (1975) and Madrid (1980–83) meetings, documents from the CSCE have shown an increase in acknowledgement of minority issues. However, efforts made by the CSCE to elaborate a definition of national minorities (last time was during the Expert Meeting on National Minorities in Geneva in the summer of 1991) always comes down to *travaux preparatoires*.

There has been a definite reluctance to conclude such a project. The main reason is that the states and their experts cannot reach a consensus on the exact definition of a national minority.[2] There is even some suspicion that the states do not

[2] *See generally*: Rosas, A., Allan, C. and Helgesen, J., *The Strength of Diversity: Human Rights and Pluralist Democracy*. Dordrecht 1991. Helgesen, J., contributed one chapter to this book, *Protecting Minorities in the Conference on the Security and Co-operation in Europe (CSCE) Process* (pp. 159–186). *See* p. 163.

wish to define the concept, so that they can delay and even complicate the work on the protection of minorities.

As far as I can understand, by reading numerous documents on national minorities, the main reason for this political unwillingness is that a clear definition of national minorities, written in an official document, might give a dangerous impetus to regional claims which have generally been satisfied by well-accepted compromises. It is true that some states, which have professed unity for several centuries, are apprehensive that a general definition might bring to the fore again regional characteristics which they have always fought against. A stringent definition would also create problems for the immigrant workers especially in Western Europe, because of the implications for national minorities. If it is clear that the question of immigrants should not be treated on the same level as national minorities, the single states are concerned about how they will organize the law in relation to all these specific topics.

It must also be emphasized that the great variety of minority groups and the difficulty of classifying them in a uniform manner is a challenge to any definition.

There are, however, attempts to find a definition which is neither too theoretical nor too abstract in its approach to the subject.

The contributions made by the CSCE in the last two decades, and more recently, by the Council of Europe, that allow at least a minimum common denominator on a definition of national minority, are important avenues for exploration and incorporation into the thinking of the most qualified international bodies dealing with minorities.

To focus on the concept of national minorities, I shall proceed with a historical analysis of the concept in our century, trying to understand the ups and downs of international concern and discussion on minorities, and shall pay special attention to the situation of national minorities after two World Wars and during "the cold war era". Looking at Europe of the

1980s, soon after the Helsinki Final Act, and taking the perspective of the documents of CSCE, I shall give evidence of the progress achieved in the intellectual definition of the concept. Finally, through the political events of our continent of 1989 and 1990, and the subsequent U.N., Council of Europe and CSCE documents, I shall try to elaborate a conceptual definition of national minority which avoids distortion by the concepts of multicultural society, cultural pluralism and minorities.

CHAPTER I

The Concept of National Minorities at the End of the First World War

Historical Precedents

The concept of national minorities *under international law has a history of only 100 years*. It was during the last century that under the specific influence of Romanticism the concept of a nation became the unifying principle for identifying a people. The 19th century was, however, already characterized by bourgeois and national development, which strengthened the desire in the various nationalities for freedom and self-determination.[1] Nonetheless, history shows that the question of minorities arose in the 16th century with the emergence of the modern state in Europe. It must be said that, since territorial sovereignty was at that time progressively replacing ethnic and cultural links, it was natural that minorities would appear, which had been separated by the frontiers of newly created states. The Powers which ruled the newly created states found themselves challenged; they reacted first by giving demonstrations of strength, then by granting minor concessions in the face of new demands.

As regards religious minorities, protection guaranteed by international agreements went back several centuries. In fact

[1] In this chapter I shall refer several times to Galántai, J., *Trianon and the Protection of Minorities*, Budapest 1992, *see* p. 5.

in the Middle Ages, Christian faith was a way of unifying people. The birth of the National States in France, Great Britain, Spain, etc. and the so-called "Renaissance", which with its different characteristics spread out almost all Europe, slowly developed and prepared the idea of a nation.

The first international treaties on the protection of minorities and the prevention of discrimination were concerned with religious rights: the Oliva Peace, concluded on May 3, 1660 in Oliva between Poland and Sweden, included a clause on the protection of a Catholic minority in Protestant Sweden. The Paris Peace Treaty, February 10, 1763 between France and Great Britain, provided religious rights to the French Catholic minority in Canada.

Only in the 19th century does a clear consciousness of minorities' rights appear which involves also other aspects of human living. The literature concerning minorities during the last century is voluminous because of very important historical events. We quote as the most important example the decisions of the Vienna Congress (1814–15). References to those decisions were made repeatedly during the Peace Conference in Paris in 1919, particularly when the division of Poland into three parts was considered. It is well known that, on the basis of this agreement, the Polish national minorities preserved their national identity and gained autonomy (although not in equal measure) in all three states. "At the Congress of Vienna, Britain proposed that the emperors who had Polish subjects should sign bilateral agreements with one another, in which they would undertake obligations enabling their Polish subjects to preserve their national identity. In May 1815, bilateral agreements were signed between Russia and Austria and between Russia and Prussia in which these powers promised to provide national institutions for their Polish subjects. On June 9, in the first paragraph of the final document signed by the eight powers participating at the Congress (Britain, Spain, France, Austria,

Portugal, Prussia, Russia and Sweden) it was stated that the Poles were to be given national representations and institutions in all three empires."[2]

The Concept of the Nation in the 19th Century

Historians generally agree that the last century brought a profound change in the concept of nation. The Enlightenment of the 18th century underlined the value of "reason". The nature of "reason" is "cosmopolitan", "universal", because the laws of reason are inherent and valid for, all humanity (French, Italians, Americans, Asians, etc.).

This concept of a nation is very close to the definition of a nation given by the Encyclopaedia, compiled at the end of the 18th century: "Nation denotes the population of a state, regardless of that population's characteristics and feelings."[3]

The Romanticism of the 19th century put its own mark on "sentiment" and "passion", realities which are special to each person. To the reformism of the Enlightenment, Romanticism opposed the revolution. "Machiavelli separated politics and religion, but in the 19th century religion has been transferred into politics, the politics became a religion. This happened for the first time in the 19th century."[4]

Under the *Ancien Régime* the fate of the nation was decided primarily by the King's military successes and defeats. National feeling might or might not develop during the process.

[2] Galántai, J., op. cit., p. 34

[3] *See* the reference to this concept, in: *The Nationalities Question—from Versailles to the Present Day*—European Teachers' Seminar, Esneux, Belgium, 18–19 April, 1991, Council of Europe—DECS/SE/BS/Sem. (91) 2, p. 1.

[4] *See* Chabot, F., *L'idea di nazione*. Bari 1961, p. 54

By the end of the 18th and during the 19th centuries (historians quoted the French Revolution in 1789 as the event which brought a new understanding of the concept of a nation) the idea of a nation coincided with the state, the latter became a national state or "nation-state".[5] The sentiment of being a nation started to be associated with the hope of creating a national state.

This means that only with a national state could the nation preserve its own identity. In fact, the concept of a nation declares the principle of the sovereignty of the people, and as a consequence, the national state is the expression of the sovereignty of the people. Each nation becomes like a tree (national state) with its root deeply attached to its own soil (nation).[6]

This new principle of nationhood is based on the conviction that any nation is entitled to aspire to set itself up as a state or join the state to which it is linked by objective affinities such as language, culture, religion.[7]

The concept of a nation during the last century was strongly supported by the idea that some fundamental characteristics are very important to keep the identity of a nation: for example, the language. "Two who speak the same language form an entity that nature has welded together in advance."[8] To lose their own language or to let another language be assimilated with their own, also means losing the "individuality" of the nation. In his "Discourse to the German Nation", Fichte defined the nation as the entity formed by all

[5] Council of Europe, DECS/SE/BS/Sem. (91), op. cit., p. 2

[6] This example is often used by several authors. *See* Chabot, F., op. cit., p. 35.

[7] Council of Europe, DECS/SE/BS/Sem. (91) 2, op. cit., p. 6

[8] This idea is mooted by J. F. Herder and taken up by J. G. Fichte in the *Reden an die deutsche Nation* (1807).

the German-speaking countries, despite their political division.[9]

As with a nation's language, religion, culture and traditions should be protected from foreign contamination. Language, religion, culture and traditions are considered the "soul" of the nation.[10]

The great national movements of the last century were dominated by deep passion which very often led to war. But if the mid-19th century revolutions in Central Europe solved, or at least pointed towards, a solution for the German, Italian, and Hungarian problems, those revolutions did not provide answers to most of the questions concerning the other nations of Central and Eastern Europe.

By the beginning of the 19th century the entire region of Central and Eastern Europe was dominated by four Empires: the Ottoman Empire, the Hapsburg Monarchy, Tsarist Russia and the Kingdom of Prussia. These four powers found themselves challenged by the passionate hopes of their subjected people. The main goal of the nationalist movements was to achieve independence and then to be an independent sovereign state.

There were two different attitudes used by the Powers in dealing with the subjected people.

At the beginning of the last century a prevalent idea was that of *concessions*, which was widely used in the 17th and 18th centuries. To solve a particular bilateral conflict, the subjected people were granted concessions. It was one way which indirectly admitted the existence of diversity among the people. Of course, the concept of concessions also meant that the subjected people were considered inferior by the leading Power State. Instead of acknowledging the specific

[9] Ibid.; *See generally*: Chevalier, J. J., *Le grandi opere del pensiero politico*, Bologna 1968, pp. 271–278

[10] *See*: Nazionalismo e Cristianesimo, in: *La Civiltà Cattolica* 3391, 5 ottobre, 1991, pp. 3–14

national values of the subjected people, the Power State only tolerated their diversity.

The concept of a nation was merely the strength of the leading Power State which would rarely acknowledge the real existence of other nations within its own borders.

The expansion of existing states, and the formation of new ones, started to be guaranteed under international law, and with the involvement of more Powers the idea of "concessions" was replaced by that of *preconditions*. "When the leading powers granted international recognition to any new state, in other words when they sanctioned them, they were entitled to insist on certain preconditions. When they recognized and guaranteed a new state, they could not be indifferent to the internal affairs of the state, for which they, too, would bear responsibility. Thus the leading powers should be entitled to impose certain obligations on the new states in connection with the national minorities living there, and to place these obligations under international law and control."[11]

The concept of preconditions was a good step towards respecting the national character of minorities. First of all, the leading Power State was no longer in a position to grant something (concession), but was obliged to acknowledge a different national group living in the same territory. The concessions were a consequence of the idea of tolerance. The preconditions were supported by the concept of protection.

During the last century the concept of tolerance was replaced by the concept of protection of the national character. It became clear that the concept of a nation is linked to a distinct group with its own ethnicity. Ethnicity can be interpreted as a sense of community based on a common heritage; history, religion, culture, race and/or language. New frontiers and the changing borders of states cannot change the national character of the people living there.

[11] Galántai, J., op. cit., p. 33

The minority protection clauses signed first in 1830 at the birth of an independent Greek state and then, in 1863, at the time of its later expansion, and above all, the resolution adopted by the Congress of Berlin in 1878, show concretely the concept of protection. In a document containing several articles, the Congress of Berlin passed a resolution with specific rules for each of the states concerned. It recognized new states (Serbia, Romania, Montenegro) guaranteeing the freedom of every citizen to profess his or her religion and to enjoy equal civil and political rights, and to be eligible for all public posts, as well as for every profession and trade. Compliance with all these rules was regarded as a necessary precondition. Only when the new, independent states accepted and satisfied these conditions did the great Powers recognize them.[12]

Studying the abovequoted documents we can easily conclude that during the last century judiciary experts and politicians were already well acquainted with the concept of a nation as a cultural entity, which had its own ethnic heritage that should be respected and protected. At the same time, it was clear that this concept of a nation was not "spontaneous" nor did it result from natural feeling, but was connected with the idea of a national state. Leaders and national movements would promote and defend the nation by war and revolution.

The awakening of national sentiment during the last century was supported by the conviction that each nation is natural and has a right to self-determination and to live independently within its own "natural" border. Also the Great Powers, involved during the last century in granting international recognition to newly created states, stood for the acknowledgement and protection of the national minorities. I can therefore say that the last century was the era which created the concept of nation, as it is understood today.

[12] *See*: ibid., pp. 33–34

The Question of National Minorities After World War I

Redrawal of the Maps of Central and Eastern Europe According to the National Concept

The problem of national minorities became acute immediately following the First World War, because of the extensive territorial reshaping which ensued and which sometimes resulted in a group losing its nationality and acquiring that of the successor state. This is why the allied and associated powers obliged a number of states, which had been their enemies during the Great War (Austria, Hungary, Bulgaria and Turkey), or which had been newly created (Poland, Czechoslovakia), or had had their territories expanded (Yugoslavia, Greece, Romania, Armenia), to enter into commitments on the treatment of minorities under their jurisdiction, and assigned specific duties to them.

The process of national re-organization in Central and Eastern Europe was sanctioned by the Paris Peace Conference with the various peace treaties concluded in 1919–20. The Principal Powers at the Peace Conference (the British Empire, France, the United States, Italy and Japan) all signed international conventions with the states touched by territorial changes (Poland, Czechoslovakia, Hungary, Romania, Yugoslavia, Greece) concerning the rights to be granted to minorities.[13]

[13] The five special Treaties expressly designed to ensure the protection of minorities (so-called Minorities Treaties) concluded with Poland (Versailles, 28 June, 1919); Czechoslovakia and Yugoslavia (Saint Germain en Laye, 10 September, 1919); Romania (Trianon, 4 June, 1920) and Greece (Sèvres, 10 August, 1920) and the special provisions in the peace treaties concluded with Austria (Saint Germain en Laye, 10 September, 1919), Bulgaria (Neuilly, 27 November, 1919), Hungary (Trianon, 4 June, 1920) and later the Treaty of Lausanne concluded with Turkey, 24 July, 1923).

The system for guaranteeing the rights of minorities developed in these treaties was particularly remarkable in that it enabled for the first time an international organization with universal ramifications as the League of Nations (the predecessor of the U.N.) to ensure the protection of minority groups.

The rights of the national minorities were reinforced by similar passages incorporated into the peace treaties. That minority rights were guaranteed under international law was regarded by the Principal Powers at the Peace Conference as an organic and indispensable element in the new state system of Central and Eastern Europe.[14]

It is worth having a quick look at the ethnic composition of Central and Eastern Europe at the beginning of this century to understand the criteria applied in deciding the nationality of individuals.

The population of Europe at that time totalled 450 to 500 million, and Central and Eastern Europe varied between 100 to 120 million inhabitants. C.A. Macartney (considered the most reliable on these topics)[15] gives in this book the population levels of the various nationalities of Central and Eastern Europe in the first decade of the century. It is interesting to note that the definition of nationality was not used in the survey: the criteria for deciding the nationality of individuals generally was the language.

The redrawing of the region after World War I is usually referred to as the formation of a system of national states. In reality, looking at the above-mentioned survey, I find that the majority of these new state formations with their multinational structures were like the preceding empires.

[14] *See*: Galántai, J., p. IX

[15] Macartney, C. A., *National States and National Minorities*, London 1934, pp. 157–178. Another survey is the one of Dr. Winkler, W., *Statistisches Handbuch der europäischen Nationalitäten*, Berlin 1931

Before 1914, half of the inhabitants of Central and Eastern Europe, some 50 million people, lived the life of minorities or subjected peoples. After the re-alignment, this number fell to 32 million, nearly one-third of the entire population of the region. The four largest states in the new power system were Poland, Romania, Czechoslovakia and Yugoslavia (Finland, even if qualified as a large state, had a low total population.)

In this sense the national concept, as a force for change, was indeed at work. Sovereignty was conferred on a number of nations which had previously had subordinate status, while other former subject-peoples became the majority in their new states. At the same time, in each of the new or enlarged countries, there were still many instances of different peoples joined together and national minorities as a percentage of the total population remained very high.[16]

The above-mentioned four states also had the largest nationality populations; it was then that the need to protect national minorities came into focus with the conviction that such protection should be based on, and guaranteed by, international law.

It seems quite clear that the concept which led to the realignment of Central and Eastern Europe at the Paris Peace Conference was the national individuality and character of each people and group according to the concept of nation that was common during the last century. In fact, in the survey of Macartney one does not find any definition of nationality. He paid special attention to language, but it is reasonable to believe that he considered as juridical practice the concept of nation and nationality as it was presented in the previous sections of this book.

I must also mention that a national concept was not the only successful one for redrawing the new borders of states. Other important criteria include economic, transport and strategic considerations.

[16] *See*: Galántai, J., op. cit., p. 13

The Concept of Nation According to the Legal Rights Granted to National Minorities

The specific problem of national minorities first arose in connection with the establishment of the League of Nations. The Peace Conference formed a committee chaired by President Woodrow Wilson. In the plenary meeting of the Peace Conference held on 31 May, 1919, President Wilson made the following statement:

"We are trying to make a peaceful settlement, and we are trying to make an equitable distribution of territories according to the race, the ethnographical character of the people inhabiting those territories.... Take the rights of minorities. Nothing, I venture to say, is more likely to disturb the peace of the world than the treatment which might in certain circumstances be meted out to minorities."[17]

President Wilson formulated his policy on minorities after having carefully calculated political considerations. I think he was convinced that for the new states greater size and larger population would represent greater strength only if the substantial minority populations thus incorporated were loyal to the sovereign power in the land. The protection of minorities was conceived in order to facilitate consolidation. This was the only way to turn minorities into real citizens and to prevent them from becoming potential enemies of the state and ensure peace.

The point of departure was that the protection of minorities was necessary in every national state inhabited by large national minorities where the character and government of that state was defined by a single ethnic group differing from the others. In a multinational state where the state was not national this kind of minority protection was not necessary (the

[17] The speech of Mr. Wilson is quoted as an Appendix Document, Appendix 1 in: Galántai, J., op. cit., pp.151–153.

U.S.A. and Switzerland were regarded as typical non-national states).

The concept of national minority at the time of the Peace Conference, according to the opinion of experts, was generally understood as a people who did not consider itself part of the majority nation and population, and as numerically inferior to the rest of the population of a state and in a non-dominant position.

With this concept, the practical propositions concerning minority rights were also restricted to some objective elements, which relate to the existence within the population, of a state of separate population groups which have stable ethnic, religious or linguistic characteristics.

The study of legal interpretation and political practice at the time of the Peace Conference is almost impossible because of the diversity of contemporary views on the subject: the various nationalities had very different demands about minority rights. But looking at various Peace Treaties concluded in 1919–20, we can group into three main categories the rights granted within the above-mentioned concept of national minorities: *1)* No discrimination between minorities and the inhabitants and nationals of the state concerned; *2)* religious and cultural autonomy; *3)* self-determination.[18]

The minimum demand in the formulation of minority rights has always been the requirement that members of a minority group should enjoy the same civil rights as any other citizen of the state. "Fundamentally equality of civil rights was the correct approach to nationality problems, but the legal and organic structure of a 'national state' could not solve the problems of the nationality composition which existed. The equality of civil rights... was no substitute for recognition of the multicultural character of a country and the establishment

[18] A study about the contemporary view on minorities rights can be seen generally in: Galántai, J., op. cit., pp. 43–51.

of a federal structure",[19] but only the acknowledgement of the reality of a minority population who encountered no more obstacles to preserve its identity.

The religious and cultural autonomy underlines the aim of preserving the special characteristic of the national minorities, concretely granting the right to create, direct and control charitable, religious or social institutions, and to establish and direct private schools. The cultural autonomy implicitly contains the concept of recognition of nationalities, including the demand for political and constitutional organization on a territorial basis for national movements.

Self-determination in this context means the right of the national minorities to organize (on the basis of territorial autonomy—which does not include the demand for sovereignty), an attainable form of self-government. Naturally not every national minority reached this point, but most of them, though not arriving at the maximum demand for self-determination, i.e. full territorial autonomy without sovereignty, achieved some sort of political right to organize themselves autonomously, from the central government.

The leading idea at the end of World War I was to progress towards the reinforcement of the national character of the new and enlarged—in reality, multinational—states. The concept of nation and nationality was always kept, not only in settling minority problems, but also in the interest of the internal stability of the states and national integration.

The right of peoples was applied for the benefit of the victors.

The protection of minorities became an organic element of the Paris Peace Treaties, even if, when the borders were redrawn in favour of the successor states, economic and strategic considerations took precedence over the ethnic principle and over the doctrine of self-determination.

[19] Ibid., p. 48

The Concept of Nation in the Context of the International Guarantees

In the re-organized Central and Eastern European belt during the years after World War I, the number of people living as members of a national minority was roughly 30 million. Most of these people became minorities as a direct result of post-war re-arrangement.[20]

Although minority problems existed all over the world during the 1920s, only conflicts involving these European minorities could threaten the world with another war. In fact, many of these minorities possessed an advanced culture and were highly aware of their national and ethnic identities.

As I said above, the system of guaranteeing the rights of minorities developed in the Peace Treaties was particularly remarkable, in that it enabled for the first time an international organization with universal ramifications, e.g. the League of Nations, to ensure the protection of minority groups. It was explicitly stated that the granting of minority rights was an *international obligation*.

In effect it had two internationally applicable guarantees: a guarantee of intangibility and a guarantee of execution.

The guarantee of *intangibility* means that the provisions for the protection of minorities could not be amended without the consent of the Council of the League of Nations. The Council would play an important part in the implementation of the guarantee. A violation of the minority protection treaties was to be classified as a dispute of international concern.[21] In such case the rules and procedures were to be classified in any conflict emerging between nations.

The guarantee of *execution* entitled the Council to have the right and the duty to report to the League of Nations any vio-

[20] *See*: Ibid., p. 110
[21] *See*: Ibid., p. 98

lation for the provision of the minorities. A Permanent Court of International Justice was established (September 1921) to rule on differences concerning the application or interpretation of these treaties.

In each case submitted to the Permanent Court, the advisory opinion was followed by a compromise in favour of the minority concerned. In general, the advisory opinion of the Permanent Court of International Justice tried to satisfy the legitimate claims of the mnorities.

"The solution or the 'suitable handling' of the minority problem in Central and Eastern Europe at that time could only be found in the relationship between the majority state and the minorities. The institution of international minority protection could help movement towards this, but the creation of such a relationship was really the task of the parties concerned."[22]

In fact, international guarantees were necessary because of the re-alignment of states in Europe. Millions of people were forced to live the life of minorities and their protection became an important element for preserving peace.

The concept of national minority at this stage was clearly understood as a people which had lost its "nationhood" and had acquired that of the successor state. The acknowledgement and the protection of the identity of those people did work well with the guarantee procedure, because the solution of the minority problem was in the hands of the League of Nations, which had a beneficial influence on the circumstances of minorities on the one hand, and on the minority policies of states on the other. The effectiveness of the system of protection should be judged by this impact.

[22] Ibid., p. 119

The Congress of European Nationalities

In 1925 the organized groups of national minorities formed an international body known as the Congress of European Nationalities which held annual assemblies in Geneva, Vienna or Berne.[23]

The Congress until 1932, contributed to European efforts to unite Europe. The Congress had two objectives: *1)* promoting the minorities' integration with the majority nations, and *2)* developing the necessary legal background.

The Congress uniting the organized national minorities of Europe was burdened with internal conflict from the beginning. There were heterogeneous groups of minorities with differing views.

The demand for cultural autonomy, which would have preserved the concept of nation, was strongly supported at the first Congress, even if some dissident groups had the opinion that the saving of the identity of a nation should be connected with territorial autonomy or even sovereignty and that cultural autonomy was not enough. This view was judged extremist and the Congress finally adopted the recommendation that a minority should aim at cultural autonomy while remaining loyal to the state it is living within.

In European states within whose borders more than one ethnic group lives, each such group should be entitled to organize legal bodies on the basis of their various conditions, be they territorial or personal, in order to nourish and promote its culture... In this right to autonomy the delegates (to the Congress) see a way in which co-operation without friction, which is based on loyalty, can be established between the minority groups of the states concerned, and also one in which links between the peoples of Europe can be promoted."[24]

[23] On the Congress of European Nationalities; *See*: Ibid., pp. 119–129
[24] Ibid., p. 124

The freedom of cultural development was a priority of the delegates at successive Congresses of European Nationalities. The idea of territorial autonomy and sovereignty was abandoned and *cultural autonomy was understood as the only way to save the concept of a nation*. The work of the second Congress was centred on the study of a theoretical foundation of the concept of cultural autonomy but without success.

However, it was out of the question that in this area of cultural autonomy the Congress of European Nationalities could provide a framework for co-operation between national minorities and the majority of the nation of the countries involved. It was clearly defined in safeguarding the territorial extension of states. The states were guaranteed their territory in return for the protection of national minorities.

The difficulties facing the various minorities in the different states testified the impossibility of finding a universally valid solution. "During the years following World War I, most of the minority groups attending the Congress of European Nationalities concentrated mainly on adjusting to the new situation and on exercising their minority rights in the given circumstances."[25] Bilateral solutions prevailed, and were considered more useful than multilateral ones.

Conclusions

The concept of national minorities during the 1920s was limited mainly to those groups who lost their nationhood as a consequence of the dismantling of the Austro–Hungarian Empire. Millions of people fell under the power of the newly created states, and the rules introduced were aimed at avoiding any tension and ensuring the stability of the frontiers which emerged after the redrawing of the map of Central and

[25] Ibid., p. 129

Eastern Europe. It should be added, however that a "uniform" approach to the concrete settlement of the concept of national minorities as it was known and accepted in the 1920s, was also impossible: what would have been an improvement for one minority group, could have been a handicap for another.

There was no attempt to create a universal prescription for minorities. The method of the League of Nations represented an extension of a long historical tradition in Europe which dealt with minority rights through treaties and declarations relating to specific groups. Key points were: *a)* recognition of the minorities; *b)* the guarantee of the rights of minorities for humanitarian and pragmatic reasons; *c)* procedures to implement the rights of minorities; *d)* treaties and declarations providing rights for all inhabitants of the states, rights for all nationals belonging to "racial, religious and linguistic minorities".

The concept of a "multinational society" was not yet assimilated into the considerations of the League of Nations, neither was the problem of the integration of large groups of people who migrated, at the beginning of the century, to the United States of America and within Europe. National minorities was a very restricted concept.

Internationally guaranteed, minority protection was mostly limited to minimum demands, although the system encouraged development within countries where the will to improve the identities of the different nationalities was present. Even if the guarantees both in written legislation and in actual practice emerged more as guarantees imposed on the defeated or newly created states than as a general concern to promote the integration of national minorities in the new states, we should admit that these guarantees in the new states of Central and Eastern Europe, greatly contributed to the successful bringing about of stability and of the assurance of peace.

As I mentioned above, at the Paris Peace Conference the decision about the borders of the new and enlarged states was the principle of nationality most followed together with economic, transport and strategic considerations.

The efforts to preserve the national identity of each group were real. An example can be taken from the opinion of the Permanent Court of International Justice: "The idea underlying the treaties for the protection of minorities is to secure for certain elements incorporated in a State, the population of which differs from them in race, language or religion, the possibility of living peaceably alongside that population and co-operating amicably with it, while at the same time preserving the characteristics which distinguish them from the majority, and satisfying the ensuing special needs."[26]

The concept of national minority resumed in the background of the 19th century. The idea underlying the Treaties for the protection of minorities was referred to those groups of nationals:

1. who, when the maps of Europe were redrawn after World War I, found themselves living outside their own state as a subject-people, numerically inferior to the rest of the population of a dominant state;
2. with three characteristics (ethnic, religious, linguistic), which were protected under a system of international guarantees.

The cultural autonomy of national minorities, which firmly included those characteristics, was supported with loyalty, as can be seen from the documentation of the Congress of European Nationalities up to 1932.

An extension of this concept of national minorities was adopted by the P.C.I.J., which in its consultative opinion of July 31st, 1930, gave a definition of the concept of minority

[26] Permanent Court of International Justice, Advisory Opinion on Minority Schools in Albania. *P.C.I.J. Reports* (AB/64) 1935, p. 17

including the three above-mentioned characteristics, but eliminating the strict interpretation of the re-alignments of the borders of states after the war. According to the International Court, minority is: "any community of persons living in a given country or locality, having race, religion, language and traditions of their own and united by the identity of such race, religion, language and traditions in a sentiment of solidarity, for the purpose of preserving their traditions, maintaining their faith, and ensuring the instruction and education of their children in accordance with the spirit of their race and mutually assisting each other".[27]

[27] Permanent Court of International Justice, Advisory Opinion on the Greco–Bulgarian Communities. *P.C.I.J. Reports* (B/7) 1930, p. 33

CHAPTER II

The Concept of National Minority in the 1930s and Soon After World War II

Protection "from" Minorities

An introductory speech delivered during the Congress of European Nationalities, held in Vienna in 1932, revealed the serious crisis that European developments caused to minorities: "In many countries the tide of chauvinism is rising, and national pride and assertion are giving way to any form of self-expression against all other nationalities".[1] It was a time when animosity between nations, once again, grew up all over Europe and the events of 1933 greatly affected the minority movements.

Since 1933, the basic attitude towards promoting minority rights and the concept of national minority changed substantially. Hitler's abuse of the protection of minorities is the main cause for this U-turn. Germany left the League of Nations in 1933. After the appointment of Hitler as Chancellor, the new German government rejected the idea of minority as a matter of principle: "Nazi ideology, based on the supremacy of one race destined to rule inferior types, could not accomodate the ideas of minority protection. According to Nazi ideology, the inferior races needed to be subjugated or even exterminated, certainly not protected".[2]

[1] *See*: Galántai, J., op. cit., p. 128
[2] Ibid., p. 133

Added to German policy towards minorities were also "anarchical factors in the Family of Nations", that pushed European politics towards a revisionist course, and the mechanism, settled soon after the First World War of dealing with minorities could no longer play an important role on the Continent.

The concept of protection of minorities was replaced by the idea of protection from minorities and the concept of nation fell into the practice of nationalism. The concept of nation is different from nationalism. The Nation has historical roots, nationalism is an ideology, an intellectual and abstract concept built on the historical awareness of being a nation.

Nationalism proclaims the absolute value of one's own nation against others. According to it, other nations should be exterminated in the name of the superiority of one's own.

Protection "from" minorities became an important element for consideration, because minorities were a challenge to the supreme value of their own nation based, according to Nazi ideology, on "blood" (*Blut*), "territory" (*Boden*) and "language" (*Sprache*). The rights of minorities were no longer recognized, and in the name of the preservation of, and in the service of, the national pride, they were slowly denied.[3]

Unfortunately, in the 1930s, these ideas were strongly proclaimed by the Nazi and the Fascist movements in Europe, minorities were increasingly isolated and we know very well the tremendous persecution against minorities, and in particular, the insane anti-Semitic measures taken.

It is also sad to note that after 1933 not only the system of international minority protection failed, but the "anarchical factors" destroyed even the co-operation established in the 1920s between the various minority movements.

In his book entitled: "International Guarantees of Minority Rights", Julius Stone, a renowned expert on problems of in-

[3] *See generally*: *La Civiltà Cattolica*, op. cit., pp. 9–10

ternational minority protection, underlined the fact that the "anarchical factors" contributed to the destruction of co-operation between the various minority movements. "We think that here, as in other vital questions of peace, there will be a long struggle against the anarchical factors in the Family of Nations, and success or failure will be constantly in the balance."[4]

The U.N.'s First Approach to the Question of National Minorities

World War II opened a new chapter in the concept of national minorities.

Comparing the situation in Central and Eastern Europe between the end of the First and the beginning of the the Second World War, we realize that at the end of the First War more than 30 million people—nearly one third of the overall population of the region—formed national minorities. This number was reduced from eight to ten million after the Second World War, or in other words, approximately 8% of the population of the area. Unfortunately, precise figures are not available, but although lacking accuracy, this still reflects the enormous changes which took place in the relative strength of majority and minority populations.

In the system established in Central and Eastern Europe after World War II, the largest national minority population was that of Hungary (approximately three million). This was followed by the German, Albanian, Turkish and Swedish minorities and an undetermined Gypsy population.

[4] Stone, J., *International Guarantees of Minority Rights.* Oxford—London 1932, p. vii

As a result of the changes, the minority issue ceased to be a problem specific to Central and Eastern Europe, and became a reality for all European countries. Justification for confirmation of all international minority protection rules for Central and Eastern Europe had disappeared. Therefore, it was stated that: "reviewing the situation as a whole, one is led to conclude that between 1939 and 1947 the circumstances changed to such an extent that, generally speaking, the League of Nations' system of international protection of minorities should be considered as having ceased to exist."[5]

As a consequence, the system for the protection of minorities, which worked quite well until 1930, was not re-established after the Second World War. A U.N. Secretariat study in 1950 concluded that the "minorities regime" had been terminated.[6]

I think that there were three important factors which also contributed to determining the new situation.

1. Most of the solutions of the minority problem after the Second World War were solved in bilateral ways to avoid tension and ensure the stability of frontiers of states.

2. A further limitation was the absence of universal scope in the rules decreed under the system of guarantees. In the 1920s the international obligation was limited only to the minimum basic rights. As I underlined in the first chapter of this book, it was left to each state to find and work out the most appropriate way for handling minority problems in a given country.

3. The Central and Eastern European system of international minority protection was replaced by negotiations and conclusions from international agreements, guaranteeing the

[5] *See*: Galántai, J., op. cit., pp. 148–151

[6] *See*: *Study of the Legal Validity of the Undertakings Concerning Minorities*. U.N.Doc. E/CN.4/1950/367

human rights of every European citizen: "while the principle of international protection of collective minority rights was increasingly losing ground, the idea of international protection of the human rights of the individual was attracting attention and sympathy".[7]

The same concept of national minorities needed a new acknowledgment considering the new historical situation. The new process started soon after the Second World War began to incorporate the specific topics of national minorities in the context of international agreements formulating universal human rights. The "old" concept of protecting particular groups had been replaced by the emergence of the "new" concept of protection of human rights of all individuals on a non-discriminatory basis.

The concept of national minority would have needed to receive universal application.

The priority accorded immediately after the Second World War to human rights did not completely relegate the rights of the national minorities to the background. But according to the new concept and international law, the obligation of the states to guarantee human rights for every citizen, included also the rights of minorities, and these rights were regarded as a universal duty.

The concept of national minority started to be considered not as a distinct topic. The reason was that soon after the war not all governments were ready to admit that national minorities did exist in their territories. In order to be able to accept the protection of national minorities, many states insisted on incorporating this subject in the larger context of human rights.

Soon after the war, the international instruments of the U.N., although not especially aimed at protecting minorities, made indirect provision for special rights for them:

[7] Galántai, J., op. cit., p. 141

1. *The Charter of the United Nations (1945)*: "The purpose of the United Nations is...to achieve international co-operation in solving international problems of an economic, social, cultural or humanitarian character, and to promote and encourage respect for human rights and for fundamental freedoms for all without distinction as to race, sex, language or religion." (Chapter 1, Article 1.3)

2. *Universal Declaration of Human Rights (1948)*: "Everyone is entitled to all rights and freedoms set forth in this Declaration, without distinction of any kind, such as race, colour, sex, language, religion, political or other opinion, national or social origin, property, birth or other status." (Article 2)

3. *General Assembly Resolution 217 C (III), entitled "Fate of Minorities" (1948)*: It was decided that the United Nations could not remain indifferent to the *fate of minorities*. The General Assembly invited the Commission of Human Rights to undertake a detailed examination of the problem of minorities, so that the United Nations could adopt effective measures to protect racial, national, religious and linguistic nationalities. The only tangible result of this study of the problems of minorities came many years later with the "International Covenant on Civil and Political Rights" (1966). I shall refer to this Covenant in the next chapter.

4. *Convention on the "Prevention and Punishment of the Crime of Genocide" (1948)*: "In the present Convention, genocide means any acts committed with intent to destroy, in whole or in part, a national, ethnical, racial or religious group." (Article 11)[8]

[8] A selection of mentioned texts can be found in the: Raoul Wallenberg Institute of Human Rights and Humanitarian Law, Report No. 17: *A Compilation of Minority Rights Standards* (printed in Sweden 1993); *See generally*: p. 97.

Soon after World War II there was a definite fear of talking openly about national minorities or of using the above-quoted documents which the U.N. had provided to protect the rights of minorities without mentioning them. I can conclude this chapter, however, with the idea that the new process started by the U.N. towards national minorities does not differ in content from the previous one. Traditionally, minorities are identified by their ethnic, linguistic and religious characteristics. These characteristics make it possible to identify very specific categories of minorities which have a certain degree of historical continuity. These three characteristics are mentioned in the first documents of the U.N. even if in the context of human rights.

CHAPTER III

The U.N. Concept of Minority

The Reluctance to Introduce the Term National Minority

In 1987, the Secretariat of the U.N. issued a compilation of proposals for the official definition of minorities which had been submitted to the U.N. over a period of 40 years.[1]

The term national minority after World War II was a source of difficulty, because it was almost impossible to give a satisfactory definition of it.

It is well known that in 1945, the Charter of the United Nations did not deal with the question of minorities. However, 21 years later, in 1966, the International Covenant on Civil and Political Rights, in Article 27, proclaimed a number of rights of ethnic, religious and linguistic minorities.

In the official documents of the U.N. the term national minorities appears only in 1992 with the Declaration on the Rights of Persons belonging to National or Ethnic, Religious and Linguistic Minorities. The current expression which the U.N. documents used to refer to a minority was "national, social or ethnic group" with the exception of the above-quoted Article 27 of CCPR.[2]

[1] U.N. Working Doc. E/CN.4/1987/WG.5/WP.1

[2] The documents quoted in this chapter, except the *Addendum* can be consulted in: Raoul Wallenberg Institute, op. cit. (texts of the U.N. documents), pp. 21–62.

For a long period the documents of the U.N. did not contain direct references to national minorities. The unwilligness of several states to accept a definition of a minority was connected with the fear that a direct reference to a minority would push them to recognize a minority as a national group, distinct from their own nationals. Several states, as a consequence of this fear, denied the existence of minorities in their own territory.

With this strong limitation, the aim of the U.N. documents was to protect the rights of minorities without arousing regionalistic claims in those states where a well-accepted compromise had been achieved.

The terminology "national, ethnic or social origin" on the one hand, helped to avoid the dangerous impetus of regionalistic claims; on the other hand, it shadowed the specific diversity of identity between the national minorities, ethnic minorities and other minorities. The deliberate reluctance to introduce the term national minority pushed the U.N. experts on the minority problem towards a distinction between minority groups and individuals who are members of minorities.

The term "national, ethnic or social origin", was more in favour of human rights for all individuals and prohibited discrimination, but was not enough to protect group rights. The national minorities would have needed more space and support in these documents on the grounds of group rights.

The lack of a distinction in the documents of the U.N. between ethnic minorities, national minorities and other minorities, contributed to create a confusion which was felt deeply in the 1990s. I think that in the U.N. documents it is possible to realize the strength of the pressure to avoid defining what was understood by minority group, and to promote new terminology which would have been closer to the real life situation of individuals belonging to minority groups. A *minority is identified in those documents by the three traditional characteristics*: ethnicity, religion and language (later also culture was included), instead of nationality. I would say that the concept of a nation was replaced by the idea of membership of a minority group. The identity of a national minority was no longer (as it was at the end of World War I) based only on the three well-known characteristics of ethnicity, religion and language, but on individual consciousness of being a member of a group with those characteristics which should be protected.

The very important change introduced by the U.N. documents was the concept that there were individuals belonging to a particular group that had to be protected, instead of the protection of a minority group itself. The consequence of this change was the distinction between a minority group and people in general. This distinction affected very much the right to self-determination, because the sovereignty of the state with its own territorial borders remains a priority, and the separation between the rights of minorities and the risk of secession became quite clear.

A distinction among minorities became more and more unnecessary because where minorities were concerned the rights of each individual were being protected.

I cannot disregard the fact that the U.N., in the context of international concern about minorities, expressed and promoted rights according to international standards towards minorities. In particular the U.N. Commission for Human Rights, with the help of international experts, tried to achieve a definition of minorities as I shall consider in the next section of this chapter. Very often the good intentions and studies of the U.N. international experts have been stopped by compromises and "escape clauses", pushed by states, that would scarcely accept their projects. Politics played an important role in the area of the definition of the rules and principles relating to minority groups.

An Attempt at a Definition of a Minority in the U.N. Special Inquiry

The efforts made by the Secretariat of the U.N. to formulate a definition of minorities have been very strong, and the question of the definition of a minority accepted at international level is still a major obstacle to the presentation of a complete system of norms to protect minorities.

In the U.N. framework for a definition it was important to research the distinction between a minority which would affirm its differences as a minority existing within the population of a state, but having separate and stable ethnic, religious or linguistic characteristics (national minorities) and a group which had been voluntarily assimilated into the national population: immigrants, workers, alien residents, etc.

This dual approach led, in 1977, Professor F. Capotorti, the Special Rapporteur of the Sub-Commission (of the Commission of Human Rights) on prevention of discrimination against and protection of minorities, to define the concept of minority as a group as follows:

1. which is numerically inferior to the rest of the population of a state and in a non-dominant-position;
2. whose members—nationals of the state—have ethnic, religious or linguistic characteristics which differ from those of the rest of the population, and who differ from the majority by virtue of language, ethnic group or religion;
3. which exhibits, even implicitly, a sentiment of solidarity for the purpose of preserving their culture, traditions, religion or language.[3]

[3] U.N. Doc. E/CN.4/Sub. 2/1977/385 rev. 1, p. 102. Special Rapporteur, F. Capotorti

The concept was confirmed in a second Report of the same Committee in 1993—Special Rapporteur, Mr. A. Eide: "a minority is any group of persons resident within a sovereign state which constitutes less than half of the population of the national society and whose members share the common characteristics of an ethnic, religious, linguistic nature that distinguishes them from the rest of the population".[4]

The approach of the two Reports is carried within the framework of Article 27 of the CCPR, but here a doubt arises on the grounds of the numerical relationship between the minority and the population as a whole. I mean, how many individuals must there be in a group before it becomes a minority? This question is important insofar as the recognition of a minority, that is numerically very small, may represent a burden on the resources of the state which is disproportionate to its size. Professor Capotorti, nevertheless, considers that this is a simple *de facto* question which should be solved case by case on the basis of the following idea: "States cannot be required to adopt special protection measures in excess of a reasonable proportionality between the effort involved and the benefit to be derived from it."[5] To justify official recognition, a minority therefore should not be too small, although it should be added that the number of the members of a minority is purely a question of fact which a definition cannot attempt to decide.

A serious task for the U.N. Committee on Human Rights was to measure and codify abstract concepts as, for example, the desire to belong to a minority group, or the common will to help preserve a cultural, linguistic or religious identity, insofar as the intensity of such sentiments, which are the product of history, are in relation to each concrete situation.

I believe that the difficulty involved in agreeing on a general definition of the term minority confined the U.N. Com-

[4] U.N. Doc. E/CN.4/Sub. 2/1993/34, p. 7. Special Rapporteur, A. Eide

[5] U.N. Doc. op. cit.—Capotorti, F.—p. 102

mittee on Human Rights to socio-cultural preferences instead of characterizing the minorities according to the various systems of guarantees mentioned in the minority treaties between the two World Wars. The characteristics referred to in those treaties made it possible to identify very specific categories of minorities which, in principle, form stable units having a certain degree of historical continuity.

All categories of minorities founded on the criteria of ethnic, religious and linguistic characteristics are always included in the U.N. documents, but especially in the latest *Addendum* on the extension of Article 27 of CCPR (I shall talk more about this in the next section) the concept of minority includes also other group categories on the basis of the idea that minority rights are individual rights of persons belonging to a group and not specific group rights.

The socio-cultural preferences needed by the working party, responsible for studying the rights of persons belonging to minorities, explain the hesitation about adding the term national minority to ethnic, religious and linguistic minorities. The addition was only recently decided with the Declaration on the Rights of Persons belonging to National or Ethnic, Religious and Linguistic Minorities (adopted by the U.N. General Assembly on the 14th December, 1992). This addition was considered necessary, because there are communities whose members have a specific cultural, linguistic and religious heritage, in given regions, and who, due to historical circumstances peculiar to them, have established their existence as national minorities. In this case the linguistic, religious or ethnic criteria are deemed insufficient to describe the minority. National minorities whose presence in a given territory is historical must also benefit from conditions necessary for the promotion and development of their identity.[6]

[6] *See generally*: Council of Europe Parliamentary Assembly AS/Jur (43) 19, 1991, p. 13

A number of experts have drawn attention, however, to the difficulty of establishing legal distinctions between national groups and ethnic groups. In the official U.N. documents this distinction is only theoretical, and national minorities are practically assimilated to other minority groups, whose members enjoy the same rights as individuals and not as groups.

The use of the term national minority is a source of difficulty since it seems impossible to give a satisfactory definition. There are three important difficulties:

1. it may, in the first instance, allude to the principle of nationalities, and in this case the difficulty is to avoid the breaking up of states (the current situation in Yugoslavia);

2. it is necessary to correct the use of the term by imposing an obligation of loyalty on minorities to the states.[7] In other cases it refers to a minority which has the nationality of a third state, and this may encourage movements of separatism;

3. finally, the term may seek to exclude from the minority protection system other minority groups, such as foreigners, who are subject to different treatment.

These three difficulties have strongly conditioned the thinking of the U.N. Committee on Human Rights and affected the concrete compilation of U.N. documents.

An answer from the Austrian Government to Professor Capotorti summarizes the pessimistic view about achieving a definition of the concept of minority: "With respect to the theoretical question raised, it may be remarked that these problems have been under discussion in the relevant literature ever since scholars started to examine minority problems. They have so far not succeeded in formulating a generally accepted definition of the concept of minority—wheth-

[7] *See*: Ibid., p. 13

er ethnic, religious or linguistic. In view of these unsuccessful efforts, it may be doubted whether a satisfactory solution of this problem is possible."[8]

Article 27 of the CCPR (1966). The Declaration on the Rights of Persons Belonging to National or Ethnic, Religious and Linguistic Minorities (1992)

Article 27 of the CCPR and the Declaration are two important documents which had a great impact on international law in the fields of human rights and national minorities. Actually the Declaration elucidates and extends Article 27 of the CCPR. It is supposed to be a guideline for "specialized agencies and other organizations of the U.N. system" (Article 9).

As I already mentioned above, the attitude followed from the early days of the U.N. towards minorities was to provide that the members of minority groups do profit from the protection of human rights in general, combined with explicit provisions against discrimination on the grounds of their ethnic, religious and linguistic background.

The general concern for human rights, combined with the prohibition of discrimination could not be more than the basis upon which to build a system of protection for minority groups in particular. However, when in the U.N. documents, I compare the protection of minorities to the rather detailed and extensive protection of human rights and fundamental freedoms of the individual in general, I find a very narrow gap.

Article 27 of CCPR was certainly a step forward in clarifying the concept of minorities. The text of Article 27 reads:

[8] U.N. Doc. E/CN.4/Sub. 2/1985/31, pp. 4–5

"In those States in which ethnic, religious or linguistic minorities exist, persons belonging to such minorities shall not be denied the right, in community with the other members of their group, to enjoy their own culture, to profess and practice their own religion, or to use their own language."

In Article 27 there are some new statements:

1. The existence of minorities as a group within the states is acknowledged.

2. Minority rights are allocated both to individuals and minority groups. Even if they are not allocated to the group itself, they are attributed to the members who should enjoy their rights with the group.

3. From a theoretical perspective, such provisions constitute more than a prohibition against the negative discrimination of minorities, and arc an acknowledgement of equality.

4. The protection of minorities is connected to the way they enjoy culture, or religion or the use of language, this practically constitutes their own identity.

5. The states have a double obligation towards minorities: *a)* to protect their particular identity; and *b)* to promote the rights connected with that identity.

The same Article 27 contains some specifications which are in line with the previous attitude of the U.N. towards minorities:

1. By not including the word national, minorities are not well identified, rather, they are assimilated by other groups.

2. The text remains more loyal to the principle of individual rights than to group rights. Individuals who belong to groups are the core concern.

3. Because of the lack of a definition of minority, Article 27 describes a *de facto* situation of groups with those characteristics.

The Declaration does not take any new step towards a definition of a minority group, but it is an important extension of Article 27, and it gives a better understanding of minority rights.

The Declaration confers on "persons belonging to national or ethnic, religious and linguistic minorities", the right to "participate effectively in decisions on the national and, where appropriate, regional level concerning the minority to which they belong or the regions in which they live, in a manner not incompatible with national legislation" (Article 2.3), and also the right to establish "contacts across frontiers with citizens of other states to whom they are related by national or ethnic, religious or linguistic ties" (Article 2.5). States are supposed to take the appropriate measures to protect and promote the identity of minorities (Article 1.1), and to "ensure that persons belonging to minorities may exercise fully and effectively all their human rights and fundamental freedoms" as well as "express their characteristics and develop their culture, language, religion, traditions and customs" (Article 4.2). The Declaration also includes a clause that pushes the states to take appropriate measures in order to give persons belonging to minorities "wherever possible" adequate opportunities to learn, or have instruction in their mother tongue (Article 4.3); and to consider appropriate measures whereby persons belonging to minorities may participate fully in the economic progress and development of their country (Article 4.4).

The Declaration takes into consideration the rapid collapse of the communist parties in the countries of Eastern Europe in 1989–90 and the sudden reappearance of nationalist phenomena. The urgent need to find constructive and peaceful solutions to this problem encountered many difficulties and the Declaration underlines the fact that peaceful solutions should try to protect also persons who belong to minorities, their identity, their rights and not only the stability of the states, their sovereignty and their borders.

The Declaration recovers the terminolgy of national minorities but still holds on to meaning the rights granted to individuals, not to groups. *The word national in the Declaration is used as group*, and is simply put together with the terminology of ethnic, religious, and linguistic (Article 2.1). The rights are granted to persons who belong to groups with these three characteristics. There is no historical reference to the concept of national minorities after World War I.

The list of rights which appears with some details explains the degree of protection granted to minorities, but the possibility of granting collective rights to minorities is still far away. The definition and the concept of a national minority was an obstacle for, and still remains hidden in, the works of the Commission of Human Rights who prepared the draft of the Declaration without being able to introduce an acceptable definition.

The Declaration deliberately avoids a clarification of the concept of minority, and does not give any idea as to how to understand the role of a minority, the problem of the citizenship of minority groups and the criteria required to be a "person who belongs to a minority group" (Article 2).

However, I must underline the fact that today the Declaration is internationally considered as the first U.N. document which establishes a common underpinning of normative practice for states dealing with minority groups or at least establishing a control activity at international level.

Addendum (1994)

According to the proposal of Article 40.4 of the CCPR, the Commission of Human Rights issued an "authentic interpretation" of Article 27 of the CCPR, with the intention of calling the states to a more exact observance of the text of the CCPR.[9]

The *Addendum* considers the rights mentioned in Article 27 of the CCRP as "individual rights", but the protection of these rights depends on the way "the minority groups keep their culture, religion or language" (Paragraph 6.2); in other words their identity. The challenge given to the states is that they should protect the rights of a person belonging to a minority group as well as the identity of the group (Paragraph 6.2). It is still not clear how the states should protect the identity of minorities as a group if their rights are those of individuals. What the *Addendum* wants to explain is that "the persons designed to be protected are those who belong to a group and who share a common culture, a religion and/or a language" (Paragraph 5.1). Therefore "the individuals to be protected need not be citizens of the state party" (Paragraph 5.1).

The interpretation of Article 27 of the CCPR underlines the fact that there are persons belonging to a minority who should be protected with respect to their identity. It means that the *Addendum* does not go further than the concept of the rights of individuals, but it is also clear that identity is something that could be enjoyed within a group.

The real extension of Article 27 of CCPR is Paragraph 5.2 of the *Addendum*. Considering the word "exist" in reference to minority groups within the states, it is not the right of the states "to determine the degree of permanence that the term 'exist' connotes. Those rights are simply that individuals belonging to those minorities should not be denied the right, in community with members of their group, to enjoy their own culture, to practise their religion and speak their language. Just as they need not be nationals or citizens, they need not be permanent residents".... "Thus migrant workers or even

[9] CCPR/C/21/Rev.1/Add.5—1994, p. 1

visitors in a state party constituting such minorities are entitled not to be denied the exercise of those rights." (Paragraph 5.2)

This new thinking, which considers as a minority group any kind of group identified generally under the well-known characteristics of ethnicity, language, religion and culture living in the state, declares the principle that, according to international law, the rights of minorities belong to individuals and their existence does not depend on the goodwill of the state where they live.

The last extension of Article 27 is connected with the self-determination right. It was already clear, according to Article 1 of the CCPR, that self-determination is a right of peoples. People in the context of the U.N. means "the permanent resident population of the territory concerned, not the separate ethnic or religious groups whether dominant or not in that territory" (Paragraph 12). The self determination right belongs only to peoples who are dominated by outside Powers.

The *Addendum*, repeating the concept that the self-determination right does not belong to minority groups, underlines the fact that the protection of a minority does "not prejudice the sovereignty and territorial integrity of a state party" (Paragraph 3.2). The right of minorities "may consist in a way of life which is closely associated with the territory and the use of its resources" (Paragraph 3.2). It means a slight acknowledgement of "internal" self-determination (like, for instance, self-government on a local basis). This is very far from any kind of real and separate right of control over the territory ("external" self-determination).

Conclusions

The documents and the practice of the U.N. are nowadays considered as a "minimum" standard already achieved by international law in dealing with minority groups.

As I mentioned above, from the documents of the U.N. new concepts of minority and of minority rights are evident. I think that the main points of the U.N. documents on the concept of minorities are:

1. The U.N. abandoned the concept of national minorities as it was expressed up to the end of World War II. Even if, in 1992, the term was used again in U.N. documents, its meaning is not clear. The reluctance to accept a definition of minority shows the tensions on this subject between politicians and experts, and the question is still open. The search for a general definition is encountering strong political reservations. Several states fear that such a definition would give a chance to a group which, at present, does not feel that it constitutes a minority, to identify itself with this definition.

2. It is clear that the rights of minority groups are promoted and protected as individual rights.

3. Minority groups are seen as groups of citizens and non-nationals who have the recognized right to be involved in the political and social life of the state where they live.

4. The protection of a minority group means a preservation of the identity of the group. The right of self-determination cannot be recognized by minorities. The autonomy of a minority ("internal self-determination") resident within a country is not seen as a right to ask for secession.

5. The concept of nationality for identifying a minority group is considered obsolete. The concept of belonging to a minority group prevails. More important than the criterion of nationality is the link and the "spirit" of belonging to a group.

6. There is no need to issue specific norms or documents for protecting a national minority, because minorities should be considered, not as national groups, but as a group of individuals with its own "group" identity.

It must also be said that the search for a general definition of the concept of national minorities in the U.N. framework is a task which cannot account satisfactorily for the extreme variety of minority groups that exist. It would seem illusory within the context of U.N. efforts to think that a generally accepted definition can be found. In fact, it seems doubtful whether a satisfactory solution for this definition is at all possible. Similarly, all efforts made in this field, within the framework of the U.N., have so far failed.[10]

[10] *See generally*: Buonomo, V., *Riflessioni in tema di tutela delle minoranze alla luce di recenti sviluppi del Diritto Internazionale* (in press), 1994. *and*: AS/Jur (43), op. cit., pp. 2–14

CHAPTER IV

The Concept of Minority in the CSCE Process

The CSCE in the Period of 1975–89

Analysing the CSCE Process in the period from 1974 until 1989, it is surprising to observe that the main positions of the three groups of the CSCE—the West, the East and the NNA (Neutral and Non-Aligned) countries—were basically not different, as regards the problem of minorities. "This was itself an extraordinary situation", due to the fact that minorities had no part to play in the European security "theatre". "To be more blunt, less academic (during the Cold War era), the minority question was not an ideal battleground for an East-West exercise."[1]

Texts adopted at the different junctures of the CSCE Process during the Cold War contain provisions explicitly addressing minority questions. However, in comparison with those relating to the protection of human rights and fundamental freedoms of the individual a large imbalance is evident. The CSCE adopted, at that time, the same attitude as the U.N. towards the minority question: the rights of the individual prevail over the needs of the minority groups.

[1] Helgesen, J., op. cit., pp. 160–161

The CSCE has been active since the Final Act of the Conference of Helsinki (1975); it was signed by representatives of 34 states,[2] and officially recognized the existence of minority problems which had to be settled for the purpose of maintaining confidence and peace in Europe.

In the Final Act there is a short and programmatic passage relating to minorities: "The participating states on whose territory national minorities exist will respect the right of persons belonging to such minorities to equality before law, will afford them full opportunity for the actual enjoyment of human rights and fundamental freedoms and will, in this manner, protect their legitimate interests in this sphere" (Principle VII, Paragraph 4). States with minorities are encouraged to apply their legislation without discrimination to persons belonging to those minorities.

"According to the recollections of the scholars, Yugoslavia wanted a reference to 'national minorities' with their mother country in another state, whereas the USSR preferred 'ethnic group'; a number of delegations, including Italy, preferred a reference to all 'minorities' which apparently included 'ideological groups'. There were difficulties over the reference to minorities as groups."[3] The main point still was how to understand the term national minority in the Final Act.

A precise definition of this key concept cannot be found in the Final Act. In the subsequent meetings within the framework of the CSCE, many efforts were made without success. A general agreement on the expression national seems to be "that the individual belonging to a minority group must be a citizen of a given state in order to enjoy that particular pro-

[2] *See generally*: Thornberry, P., *International Law and the Rights of Minorities*. Oxford 1992, pp. 248–254

[3] *See*: Ibid., p. 252

tection".[4] An interpretation of the national minority restricted only to those groups with "their mother country in another state" cannot be based on Principle VII, Paragraph 4. At the same time, it must be said that the same Principle does not cover the new wave of minority groups in Europe: migrant workers, refugees, etc.

If we compare the above-mentioned Principle with Article 27 of the CCPR, we find that the concept national was not included in Article 27, and it might be said that the term "minorities" has a broader meaning which would not exclude newly settled groups on the territory from the protection offered under Article 27. The narrower restriction of the concept of minorities in the Final Act does not affect the concept of "existence" expressed in both documents. "Existence should be interpreted in a factual sense: minorities are not born or extinguished simply through some act of their host state."[5]

The other reference to national minorities in the Final Act is in the part of the "Basket-Three": "National minorities or regional cultures". "The participating states, recognizing the contribution that national minorities or regional cultures can make to co-operation among them in various fields of culture, intend, when such minorities or cultures exist within their territory, to facilitate this contribution, taking into account the legitimate interests of their members". The idea is that contacts between groups would promote better understanding, which in turn would perhaps lead to a reduction in political tension between states. This indicates clearly that the cultural co-operation between minority groups is something different from that of the majority population.

The fact that culture is recognized as a specific criterion, distinguishing a member of a minority group from a member

[4] Helgesen, J., op. cit., p. 163
[5] Thornberry, P., op. cit., p. 253

of a majority group, seems to weaken the argument that the cultural co-operation should also involve "external" cultural relations between majority and minority groups and between national minorities and their mother country. The culture of minorities is not well elaborated in the Final Act.

However, it should be noted that "this Paragraph ('Co-operation and Exchanges in the Field of Culture') is not contained in the Declaration on Principles and is clearly, as evidenced by the terminology, part of the political 'soft-law' aspect of the Final Act and amounts to a declaration of will or intent of States rather than a statement of obligation".[6]

Although the national minorities are not explicitly mentioned in Principle VIII: "Equal rights and self-determination of peoples", this Principle has an important relevance for those minorities which qualify for recognition as a people. The Final Act does not give an explicit definition of the term "people", but, according to established interpretation within the U.N. context, the term "people" refers to a population which does not live dispersed all over the territory of a state, nor in enclaves in the territory. In the Final Act, the concept of people should be interpreted as in the U.N. framework. The right of self-determination cannot be applied to minorities, even if the problems of so-called "external" self-determination of minorities (right to separatism, to secession, to form a separate state) cannot be solved by a reference to Principles III and VIII: "Inviolability of Frontiers", of the Final Act.

Of course Principles III and VIII "do not exclude the change of frontiers as a result of negotiations, conducted between a state and a minority group. The main implication... is that the states—in their common interest—will be reluctant to provoke or to encourage secessionist movements based purely on minority criteria".[7] In contrast to the 1960s, when

[6] Ibid., p. 252
[7] Helgesen, J., op. cit., p. 167

many "peoples" were granted the right to form separate states, the situation within the CSCE was supported by a strong scepticism about any separatism or efforts to promote secession by minority groups from the mother state.

In summary, the provisions of the Helsinki Final Act are a welcome recognition of the relevance of minorities for the agenda of international relations.

The negative point of Principle VII, Paragraph 4 is that a definition of national minorities should have been included.[8] In fact, Paragraph 4 contains many elements which are important for a definition. It is the first time after World War II that in an international forum, the protection of national minorities is clearly highlighted, in the sense that the Final Act recognizes that rights can be exercised even in common with other members of the group. The rights of national minorities are protected as group rights and the loyalty to individual rights remains untouched. To reach a compromise among delegations (some of them "would accept nothing more than a text in which the individual members of minority groups enjoy basic human rights, as do all other individuals in the respective state"),[9] the definition of national minorities was not included, but the main elements of what national minorities are were described.

The Concluding Document of the Vienna Meeting (15 January, 1989)

Analysing the protection of the rights of minorities according to the Vienna Concluding Document, one perceives the efforts made to identify some of the criteria qualifying individu-

[8] *See*: Carrascosa Coso, A., *La Santa Sede y la Conferencia sobre la Seguridad y la Cooperación en Europa*, Cuenca 1990, p. 211

[9] Helgesen, J., op. cit., p. 163

als as belonging to minority populations under: "ethnic, cultural, linguistic and religious identity" (*Article I, Paragraph 18.19*).

This was certainly not a definition of the concept of a national minority, but comparing the provisions of the Vienna Document with the "Human Contacts" part in the Final Act, it is easy to realize that the Final Act does not contain texts which establish contacts "through travel and other means of communication, including contacts with citizens of other states with whom they share a common national origin or cultural heritage" (III.1). This change does not represent a change of substance, but it is an extension of the provisions of the Final Act (which makes no mention of any "right to an identity") in order to clarify the right to an identity of national minorities.

The Vienna Document spells out the necessary measures (legislative, administrative, judicial and other) to emphasize the responsibility devolving on every state to make the protection of minorities a living reality.

In conclusion, I would underline that the text of the Vienna Document mainly re-iterates rights already expressed in previous CSCE documents or in other international instruments, but at the same time it is an important step towards a better understanding of the concept of national minorities especially as regards their identity.

In the Cold War period was the CSCE too cold on the definition of a concept of minorities? "One has to keep in mind that the founding fathers of the CSCE, and particularly of the Final Act, imagined no active role for minority groups. In retrospect, this might be claimed to be optimistic at best, and naïve at worst."[10] At the same time, one has to realize that, since the first approach to the minority question, in the framework of the CSCE, the term national minority (which applies only

[10] Ibid., p. 165

to a specific category of minorities distinct from other minorities) has been retained. I find a difference between Article 27 of the CCRP and the Final Act as regards attitude towards the meaning of the concept of a minority.

As I shall show in the next section, the events of 1989 and 1990 in Europe, saw the emergence again of the minority conflicts that were frozen during the communist dictatorship in Central and Eastern Europe. These have given the CSCE a new and more motivated commitment to study minority problems in greater depth, and to try to make progress in defining the concept of national minority.

The CSCE Process in the New Europe (1990s)

The Conference on the Human Dimension of the CSCE (Copenhagen, 29 June, 1990)

The Vienna Document was the introduction to a series of meetings called "the Conference on the Human Dimension". The Conference comprised three meetings held in Paris, Copenhagen and Moscow, respectively.

The Copenhagen meeting reflected the new political climate in Europe. The political atmosphere was totally changed. The representatives of the "new" democratic regiones, those of at least some of the "old" democratic regimes, the representatives of so many non-governmental organizations (NGO) were for the first time discussing together the establishment of a standard of rights for minority populations.

Chapter IV of the Copenhagen Document is completely dedicated to the protection of minorities.

"Some delegations wanted to open a full discussion on the concept of 'national minority'. The reason for this initiative was not only to reach intellectual clarity, but also to try to expand the definition of those categories of minorities falling within the preview of the CSCE regulations."[11] The problems of migrant workers in Western Europe touched some delegations who were requesting provisions for "guest-workers" in the context of the protection of minorities. This opinion was widely contested because the problems of migrant workers should not be treated at the same level as that of the national minorities.

The CSCE states failed to achieve consensus on a definition of national minorities. "Who belongs to a national minority was solved in a very voluntaristic way":[12] "To belong to a national minority is a matter of a person's individual choice and no disadvantage may arise from the exercise of such choice." (Paragraph 32.4)

However, the subjective criterion is not the only nor an exclusive one. "The main consequence of the quoted passage is that it is not up to the majority to decide whether an individual should be permitted to join a minority group... no formal registration by authorities is required."[13] In the same Paragraph it was also written that persons belonging to a national minority have the right "to establish and maintain unimpeded contacts among themselves within their country as well as contacts across frontiers with citizens of other states with whom they share a common ethnic or national origin, cultural heritage or religious belief" (Paragraph 32.4). "This agreement banned the 'traditional' East European practice of prohibiting contacts between members of national minorities across frontiers (e.g. contacts between the Hungarian minority in Romania and citizens of Hungary)."[14]

[11] Ibid., p. 172

[12] *The Conference on Security and Co-operation in Europe, Analysis and Basic Documents, 1972–1993*. Ed. by A. Bloed, Dordrecht 1993, p. 94

[13] Helgesen, J., op. cit. 174.

[14] *The Conference*, op. cit., p. 94

I have already mentioned that minority rights in the Final Act are mostly understood as "person" rights. The Copenhagen Meeting avoids discussing the issue of individual rights and group rights, and the Document states: "Persons belonging to national minorities can exercise and enjoy their rights individually as well as in community with other members of their group" (Paragraph 32.6). Comparing this text with Article 27 of the CCPR: "Persons belonging to such minorities shall not be denied the right in community with the other members of their group to enjoy...", we find a similarity of approach, which privileges individual rights. Subjects who carry the right are the: "Persons belonging to a minority". When the Copenhagen Document was drafted, the attitude towards group rights was not favourable. After the events of 1989 and 1990, scepticism towards collective human rights increased. It should also be noted that both documents (Article 27 and Paragraph 32.6) recognize, beyond doubt, that the right to belong to a minority is also a collective right, seen "in community with the other members of their group".

When the Copenhagen Document is compared with the Final Act, a step backward can be seen because it emphasizes the individualistic character of a minority, but there are also signs of a step forward, since this document recognizes more openly that minority rights can be exercised in common with other members of the group.

The participation of minorities in social life is covered in the Copenhagen Document with a clear principle of territorial integrity of states (Paragraph 37). The concessions for local or autonomous administrations (Paragraph 35) are elements which connect with the principle of self-determination in its "internal" aspect, this means a kind of self-government on a local basis. Any rights of separatism and secession are clearly excluded.

The obligatory character of the provisions of the Copenhagen Document is submitted to a great number of "escape clauses". Often CSCE states only pledge to "endeavour" or to "consider" and in the case of possible autonomous administrations of minority (Paragraph 35) states are only prepared to "note". Two CSCE states (Greece and Bulgaria) felt obliged to submit interpretative statements. For our purpose the Bulgarian statement is interesting because it emphasized the domestic jurisdiction of states in dealing with national minorities *whenever they exist.*[15]

If one considers the Copenhagen Document by comparison with what has been done over many years on minorities, the outcome is surprising.

Looking closely at the Copenhagen Document, *the only unanswered question* was a clear definition of the concept of national minorities. However, Chapter IV of the Document is a major achievement with regard to the concept of national minorities, especially concerning identity and rights proclaimed as individual and group rights. All the provisions of the Copenhagen Document refer strictly to national minorities, without extension of these provisions to other minority groups (migrant workers).

The Charter of Paris for a New Europe (21 November, 1990)

The Paris Charter, which was signed on 21 November, 1990 by all the heads of state or government, communicates a spirit of optimism. It officially declared that the "era of confrontation and division of Europe has ended" and that "ours is a time for fulfilling the hopes and expectations our peoples have cherished for decades" (introduction). "The degree of violent ethnic-based conflicts that were soon to emerge in various

[15] *See*: Ibid., p. 95

places within the CSCE area, was evidently not expected at the time of the Paris Summit."[16]

The chapter on "Guidelines for the Future" states: "Determined to foster the rich contribution of national minorities to the life of our societies, we undertake further to improve their situation". In this context it was decided to convene an experts' meeting on national minorities in Geneva in July 1991.[17]

The few lines of the Charter of Paris for a New Europe dedicated to national minorities are important because they show a new approach to this question, based on the fact that the minorities do play a role in the future of Europe, particularly in the fields of political stability and military security.

Experts Meeting on National Minorities (Geneva, 19 July, 1991)

In July 1991, a year after the Copenhagen Meeting, the situation of minorities in Europe gave serious cause for worry to the delegations. The urgent crisis in Yugoslavia had a negative impact on the Geneva Meeting. The unity of the national state was more than ever threatened. The negotiating climate in Geneva was therefore extremely realistic. One statement of the text of the "Contribution of the Council of Europe to the Meeting" summarizes the general mood of the meeting: "On the one hand... it is clear that general solutions, particularly in the standard-setting field, can only have the character of minimum standards and give guidance to the solution of minority problems. This is due to the special features of each minority situation. On the other hand the promotion of the linguistic, religious, cultural and social identity of minorities

[16] Ibid., p. 61
[17] Ibid., p. 61

should not entail the risk of undermining political stability and social peace, either within or between the countries concerned."[18]

Due to the sensitive nature of the subject concerned, the meeting did not achieve any impressive result. The major questions remained unsolved.

Efforts were made to elaborate on a definition of the concept of a national minority. The participating states did not reach agreement on the question of defining a national minority. "The CSCE states could not reach agreement on the question whether national minorities should be granted collective rights. For a number of CSCE states this would have implied a danger of separation of their minorities from the state."[19]

Some delegations underlined the fact that the latest CSCE documents on minority questions had gone too far.

The Report of the Geneva Meeting is rather vague and enumerates a number of principles which should guide the treatment of national minorities. All the previous CSCE documents on national minorities were fully confirmed. In this way the Experts' Meeting does not deviate from previous declarations on national minorities and its most important achievement was the following statement: "Issues concerning national minorities, as well as compliance with international obligations and commitments concerning the rights of persons belonging to them, are matters of legitimate international concern and consequently do not constitute exclusively an internal affair of the respective state. They note that not all ethnic, cultural, linguistic or religious differences necessarily lead to a creation of national minorities" (II).

[18] Council of Europe, Contribution of the Council of Europe to the CSCE Meeting of Experts on National Minorities, Geneva, 1–19 July, 1991, pp. 4–8

[19] *The Conference*, op. cit., p. 98

This statement cannot be seen as a commitment in a strict sense, but it certainly halted the attempt to restrict minority issues to an internal question of a national state, and to underline the specific character of a national minority.[20]

The Conference on the Human Dimension of the CSCE (Moscow, 3 October, 1991)

The meeting was influenced by the dramatic event of the *coup d'etat* against President Gorbachev. The Moscow Document deals with items of human rights, but no progress was possible on the highly topical question of international protection of the rights of national minorities. Any attempt to try to reopen the issue of minorities failed completely. "In particular some Western delegations, e.g. France, Greece and Turkey, blocked any significant progress in this field."[21] Other delegations felt that sufficient attention had already been devoted to national minorities.

Many delegations show great reluctance to solve the question of the concept of national minorities with concrete statements and the conflicts connected with minority affairs in general.

The Helsinki Follow-up and Summit Meeting: The Challenges of Change (10 July, 1992)

The Helsinki Document differs from the Charter for a New Europe of November 1990. "The Paris Charter was phrased in very optimistic terms, looking forward to a bright new future

[20] *See*: Helgesen, J., op. cit., pp. 180, 183

[21] *The Conference*, op. cit., p. 96

after the collapse of communism in Eastern Europe...The Helsinki declaration reflects a quite different mood, referring to serious difficulties and disappointments."[22]

The text on the problems of national minorities "is on the effective implementation of existing commitments rather than on additional substantive obligations".[23]

A major success of the Helsinki Meeting was the establishment of the new post of CSCE:

High Commissioner on National Minorities (HCNM)

It should be observed that the mandate of the HCNM is rather vague. Concepts, such as "early warning" or "tensions" or "potential to develop into conflict" have to be defined.

The institution of the HCNM is a specific instrument to prevent conflicts involving national minorities at the earliest possible stage, to identify the underlying causes of tensions, and to try to resolve them before they escalate.

The HCNM is not in charge of the promotion and protection of the rights of national minorities, but rather is concerned only to deal with situations of "early warning".[24]

Even if the mandate of the HCNM is limited in many ways (it should take action only in regard to tensions which have developed beyond an early warning stage—Chapter II, Paragraph 3—it will not communicate with, and will not acknowl-

[22] Ibid., p. 63

[23] Helgesen, J., op. cit., p. 185

[24] For notes on the current work of the High Commissioner *see*: Huber, K.J. and Zaagman, R., Towards the Prevention of Ethnic Conflict in CSCE: The High Commissioner on National Minorities and Other Developments. *1st International Journal of Group Rights* 1 (1993), pp. 51–58

edge, communications from any persons or organizations which practise or publicly condone terrorism or violence—Paragraph 25), the creation of the HCNM is a promising step. He could enhance a process of exchange of views and co-operation between the states for facilitating a better and clearer understanding of the concept of national minorities with the questions connected with this definition (identity, collectivity, relationship with other minority groups).

Seminar on National Minorities (Warsaw, 24–28 May, 1993)

The Seminar focused on the positive solutions to national minority problems. Although the HCNM's mandate was formulated in terms of conflict prevention, his participation in the Seminar shows a close link with the CSCE Human Dimension.

The discussion on the definition of the concept of national minorities was very interesting even if it received no acknowledgement in the document. The Seminar focused on the political monitoring mechanism of the CSCE and the ways in which it could be improved.

The discussion on the definition of a national minority took place in Group 1 and could be summarized as follows: "One has to be aware of the fact that terms such as 'minority', and especially 'ethnic group', have negative connotations in the former communist countries, while we should strive for a neutral and descriptive usage applied in the CSCE context. Also the discussion stressed the need for an understanding of minorities, human rights and minority rights on a non-territorial basis when dealing with dispersed minorities (without their own territory, e.g. the Gypsies), and as a consequence the necessity of elaborating more on the possibilities of using an individual's personal identity and personal choice of identity as a foundation for defining all types of minorities."[25]

This report shows how important it is to be clear in terminology, in order to achieve a better understanding of the identity of national minorities. In this particular subject political fear prevails and the achievement of a definition of the concept of national minorities seems as far away as ever.

It is interesting to note that the Netherlands, on the protection of national minorities "recommended that the impressive results achieved within the CSCE be co-ordinated with the work of the Council of Europe and the U.N" (see Chapter 3, Paragraph b).

I consider that this recommendation deserves very serious attention, because co-operation between the CSCE, the U.N. and the Council of Europe is the only way to bring more concrete and binding results to the protection of national minorities in general and to the study of a definition of national minority in particular.

Conclusions

Documents emerging from the CSCE on national minorities show a new way of thinking. From the early days of the U.N. the perspective was an individualistic one: a member of a minority group was protected as an individual, not as a member of a minority group. The new thinking of the CSCE Process is based on the acceptance of the term national minority and on the fact that national minorities should be protected both as group and as individuals.

[25] *CSCE Human Dimension Seminar on Case Studies on National Minorities: Positive Results, Warsaw, 24–28 May, 1993*, Discussion Group 1, Report from the Sub-group on dispersed minorities, e.g. Roma—by Helen Krag, Denmark, p. 2

Since the Final Act of Helsinki there has been a marked growth in the acknowledgement of minority issues.

I suggested that the analysis of the CSCE Process be done in two periods: the first from 1975–89 (the Cold War) and the second from 1990–94 (The "new, pluralist Europe").

The provisions established in the CSCE Process show the different general approaches adopted towards national minorities.

First of all the term national minority constantly recurs in all the CSCE Documents. This is a clear sign of the particular attention given to this specific topic. National minorities are not assimilated or confused with the so-called new wave of minority groups. Even if a definition of national minority has not been reached up to now, within the framework of the CSCE, great efforts have been made to elaborate a definition of this concept (last time during the Seminar on National Minorities in Warsaw, 1993). I would say that in analysing the CSCE Process, it can be clearly understood which groups are not national minorities, and at the same time it is possible to deduce some specific rights reserved to them.

In the first period of the CSCE Process the rights of the national minorities are presented primarily as group rights. At the Copenhagen Meeting (1990) the terminology of Article 27 of the CCPR returns: "Persons belonging to national minorities". It is beyond doubt that in both periods of the CSCE Process, even if with different emphasis, the rights of national minorities are clearly understood as collective and individual rights. Persons can exercise these rights in the group or outside the group to which the "person belongs". "To belong to a national minority is a matter of individual choice." (Paragraph 32.4 of the Copenhagen Conference, 1990)

The concept of national minority in the CSCE Process recalls the historical definition generally accepted at the end of World War I and based on the awareness of the recognition of the right of a different group, living in the same territory, in a non-dominant position, with its own particular identity. This identity needs to be protected. In this context the following statement is a promising step: "Persons belonging to a national minority have the right to establish and maintain unimpeded contacts among themselves within their country as well as contacts across frontiers with citizens of other states with whom they share a common ethnic or national origin."[26] (Copenhagen Document)

The statement, that the authorities should play an active part in protecting and promoting this identity (Copenhagen Document), also breaks new grounds.

The list of rights granted to national minorities within the CSCE Process has direct relevance to all the crucial questions concerning security and co-operation in Europe: security, self-determination, territorial integrity, political participation, rule of the law, protection of human rights.

Innovative procedures do not *per se* provide a guarantee that international actions will become more effective. The reluctance to accept a definition of the concept of national minority shows that "too frequently the primary concern of governments is the potential disruption or subversion which they expect as a result of too effective a minority assertion".[27] The practice of the CSCE Process teaches that governments assume that a definition of national minorities, which would admit a preferential treatment to groups, would fuel secessionist claims, threatening the national unity, political independence and territorial integrity of states.[28]

This reluctance towards a definition of the concept of national minorities is further demonstrated in the fact that procedures are not always accessible to the concerned minority groups, or when decisions have been taken, they are blocked at the political level.

[26] *The Conference*, op. cit., p. 94
[27] Helgesen, J., op. cit., p. 76
[28] *See generally*: AS/Jur (43), op. cit., pp. 9 and 19

The establishment of the post of the HCNM is very promising, in particular in the prevention of conflict from the outset. But I think that the most successful result of the establishment of the HCNM is that his intervention would promote a better understanding of national minorities and that the international community should respond to their expectations even if there is no conflict.

Limitations of the various CSCE Documents could derive from the fact that any document adopted under the CSCE process has no legal value. "This observation should not, however, be taken to imply that the CSCE Documents are not binding. The binding force of these documents is not seriously doubted."[29] The fact that these documents are not legally binding agreements has not affected their political authority.

I refrain from entering into a complicated debate on the difference between binding and non-binding agreements, because it has very little practical consequence on the results that can be expected from states. Nevertheless, I wish to underline that the CSCE Documents reflect a consensus on protecting the national minorities' rights and mark a progress on the research for constructive solutions to the problems of minority rights.

The CSCE Documents on national minorities had a resounding success on the agenda of international relations. In the field of security and co-operation in Europe (which is exactly its main mandate) the attention given to national minorities is a great contribution, particularly to the European states when they describe particular groups in their constitutions, or when they establish bilateral or limited multilateral treaties.

The discussion on the concept of national minorities should continue in a context of co-ordinated debate with the work of the Council of Europe and the U.N.; this would seem to be the only way (suggested also in the Warsaw Seminar on National Minorities, 1993) to achieve a concrete result in this matter.

[29] *The Conference*, op. cit., p. 22

CHAPTER V

The Concept of Minority in the Context of the Council of Europe

In the Council of Europe several stages can be identified in the minority issue.

Since its creation the Council of Europe has been attentive to problems arising from the existence of minorities in Europe.

In 1949, the Commission on legal and Administrative Affairs of the Consultative Assembly unanimously recognized the importance of the minority problem. However, it was not until 1956 that it really started the work, following a reminder from the Assembly that a more accurate definition of the rights of minorities was essential.[1]

The European Convention on Human Rights and Fundamental Freedoms (1950)

The term national minority appears in Article 14 of this Convention, in the context of the protection of human rights. In many ways the human rights recognized for all individuals (freedom of thought, conscience, religion, expression, peace-

[1] *See*: AS/Jur (43), op. cit., pp. 4–5

ful assembly) are also applied to national minorities. Article 14 states that "the enjoyment of the rights and the freedoms set forth in this Convention shall be secured without discrimination on any grounds such as sex, race, colour, religion, political or other opinion, national or social origin, association with a national minority, property, birth or other status".

In fact, this is the only legally binding international regulation to date in the field of minority protection. Article 25 recognizes the rights of minorities as a "group of individuals" to bring petitions before the European Commission of Human Rights.

The first approach of the Council of Europe is very similar to that of the U.N. In line with the Universal Declaration of Human Rights, the Convention does not contain specific provisions for minorities, though unlike the Universal Declaration, the Convention employs the term minority. It should be obvious that there is not a clear concept of national minority. The Convention is structured on the rights of individuals and not on collective rights: it does not focus on minorities. These are assimilated into a "group of individuals" who have the right to enjoy what is stated in the Convention. Even if some of these rights can be exercised in a community, there is no guarantee in the Convention for the enjoyment of these rights in a community.

The term national minorities in this Convention was ambiguous, because it was not supported by any specifications which would have saved a particular identity with reference to the historical background that is beyond this term. In the context of Article 14, the expression cultural minority would have been more understandable than national minority. In fact, the protection of so-called cultural rights needed to be supplemented by additional provisions which should preserve the right to enhance the characteristics of the specific cultural life of the national minorities.

Nevertheless, the importance of the Convention lies in two main factors: in the scope of the rights protected and in the machinery of protection established to investigate alleged violations and to ensure respect for the obligations under the convention. As regards the machinery of protection (Article 25), it is established that *"a group of individuals can also claim to be victim of a violation of human rights"*. Experts have seen in this statement a kind of collective guarantee for the respect for human rights recognized in the Convention.

The possibility of an article or an additional protocol has engaged the attention of commentators since the Convention was drafted. I shall consider only those proposals strictly relevant to a definition of the concept of national minorities.

What does the term national minority mean in the Convention? An answer to this question came with *Recommendation 285* (1961) to which the Committee of Ministers was invited to include in the Additional Protocol to the European Convention on Human Rights an Article designed to guarantee national minorities. The draft of the Article was as follows: "Persons belonging to a national minority should not be denied the right in community with the other members of their group, and as far as compatible with public order, to enjoy their own culture, to use their own language, to open their own schools and to receive education in the language of their choice and to profess and practise their own religion."[2]

Recommendation 285 of the Parliamentary Assembly described the term national minorities as non-dominant groups being aware of belonging to a national minority. The awareness is based on the identity of the groups. But the above-quoted text, prepared on that occasion, which provided specific "collective rights" to be shared with other members of their group, was not included in any protocol.

In the early 1960s when the question of the collective rights of national minorities came up, a fundamental problem

[2] Doc. 1299, 26 April 1961. *See generally*: AS/Jur (43), op. cit., p. 5, note n. 10

blocked the "official" recognition of group rights: the conviction that the Convention for the protection of Human Rights covers only individual rights, in view of the fact that these rights are obviously matters of collective right. I do believe that this conviction was also based on two considerations: *a)* the negative response of the Committee of Experts which, interpreting the purpose of the Convention, saw no need to introduce an Additional Protocol. Officially it was decided to defer the issue; *b)* an influence of the "Struye Report" submitted to the Assembly in April 1959,[3] which concluded that the status of minorities in Western Europe was fairly satisfactory.

In conclusion, I would underline the fact that the Convention includes several provisions which are important for the protection of national minorities. Moreover, Article 14 contains a non-discrimination clause which provides that the enjoyment of rights and freedoms recognized in the Convention must be guaranteed without any distinction to *inter alia* members of a national minority.

The Council of Europe on National Minorities During the 1970s and 1980s

Reasons of a political nature contributed to a slowdown in the process of preparing an Additional Protocol to the Convention with special provisions for protecting national minorities, which would have solved or at least discussed the delicate question of collective rights. No specific recommendations or declarations on national minorities were made in these decades. The approach to the question of minorities became more and more "pragmatic". The Committee of Experts

[3] Doc. 1002, 30 April 1959. *See also*: AS/Jur, op. cit., p. 5

stated in 1973 that an Additional Protocol was legally unnecessary.[4]

In mid-1970 the attention of the Council of Europe was drawn to the cultural aspect. Several bodies of the Council looked into the matter of modern languages in Europe, which is still one of the most sensitive issues addressed in minority demands, and certainly the concept of the rights of linguistic minorities should be included in collective rights.

Recommendation 814 (1977) of the Parliamentary Assembly on "modern languages in Europe" stated the principle that linguistic and cultural rights should be safeguarded because cultural diversity is an irreplaceable asset. "The European Charter on Regional and Minority Languages" (approved only in 1992 as I shall refer to it later) re-affirms the right of peoples to express themselves in their regional or minority language both in their private and social lives.

Two important Reports (prepared in the context of the European Parliament) concerning national minorities, minority languages and cultures were taken as a guide to adopt recommendations or resolutions in these matters even for other European bodies.

The first Report, known as the "Arfé Report 1981", was prepared to design a Community Charter of regional languages and cultures and a Charter of the rights of ethnic minorities.[5] The second, known as the "Stauffenberg Report—1988"[6] was prepared to establish the rights of ethnic groups

[4] The Council of Europe and Minorities, CoEMIN, September 1994, p. 25; *See also*: Doc. DH/Exo (73), 9 November, 1973

[5] Report on a Community Charter of regional languages and cultures and a Charter of the rights of ethnic minorities (1981): Rapporteur, G. Arfé, Doc. PE, 1981/965

[6] Draft report on a Charter establishing the rights of ethnic groups living in member states of the European Community. Part A: proposal for a resolution. Rapporteur, F. L. Stauffenberg, 17 March, 1988, PE 121.212. *See generally*: AS/Jur (43), op. cit., p. 6

living in member states of the European Community. Even if these two Reports are not strictly connected with the Council of Europe, I quote them because of the philosophy which subtends these texts. The main idea is that the unity of Europe must be more than a market unity, and that this is possible only if the existing cultural pluralism, which is the source and the expression of its wealth, is respected. This simple statement expresses an important principle for the adoption of adequate legal regulations on minority rights in the 1990s.

Stauffenberg also gives a definition of the concept of national minorities with the exclusive help of objective criteria, introducing at the conceptual level new elements such as *generation* or *territory*. Beneficiaries of the rights are groups of individuals or minorities whose presence in a member state has been a matter of fact for a number of generations; who differ from an ethnic, religious and/or linguistic point of view from the rest of the population; who have a specific cultural identity and who constitute a demographic minority in that state. The draft also offers definitions of the expressions "members of an ethnic group" and "ethnic region". The first concerns all persons reclaiming their membership of an ethnic group as long as they do not contest this; the second refers to the well-defined territory and scattered pockets in which ethnic groups have been established for a long time.

The Council of Europe on National Minorities in the 1990s

Recommendation 1134 (1990)

In the spring and summer of 1990, Europe changed dramatically and the question of the protection of national minorities became extremely urgent. Heads of states and experts felt that peace and prosperity could only be maintained in Europe if ways of enabling the different ethnic, linguistic and religious communities to live together within common frontiers could be found. With this conviction the Parliamentary Assembly of the Council of Europe adopted the so-called Recommendation 1134 "on the rights of minorities", which represents a very important statement especially because of its influence on other working documents of the Council.

The Recommendation stresses that "respect for the rights of minorities and persons belonging to them is an essential factor for peace, justice, stability and democracy" (Article 4).

The distinction between different kinds of minorities in Europe is underlined in Article 1. "There are many kinds of minorities in Europe. They have certain characteristics which may be ethnic, linguistic, religious or others which distinguish them from the majority in a given area or country."

A definition of the concept of national minorities even if it is not clearly stressed, can be easily deduced in Article 11: "National minorities—that is to say, separate or distinct groups, well defined and established in the territory of a state, the members of which are nationals of that state and have certain religious, linguistic, cultural or other characteristics which distinguish them from a majority of the population". The rights recognized to them are also collective rights "national minorities shall have the right to be recognized as such by the states in which they live". National minorities are understood as nationals of the state (Article 11).

Among the basic principles on the rights of minorities in general, minorities are "allowed to have free and unimpeded peaceful contacts with citizens of other states with which they share a common origin or heritage, without, however, infringing the principle of the territorial integrity of states" (10. iv).

Recommendation 1134 concluded by proposing to the Committee of Ministers that it draw up a Protocol for the European Convention on Human Rights or hold a special

Council of Europe Convention to protect the rights of minorities (Article 17).

The principles stated in the Recommendation show the new approach started with the 1990 events of the Council of Europe for the protection of minorities. "The Recommendation does not contain a full catalogue of minority rights, but it is rather a reconnaissance of the content and structure of possible instruments."[7]

There are rights ascribed to groups (collective) and rights for individuals.

The awareness of the Council of Europe of being the European organization having the greatest authority in the field of human rights (which admitted all the countries of Central Europe to membership), gave successful results for the practical recognition of national minorities and their protection.

The so-called pragmatic approach of the Recommendation underlines the fact that those principles should not remain only on paper but should be slowly introduced into a context of national laws.

The Venice Commission

The European Commission for Democracy through Law (known also as the Venice Commission), a consultative body of the Council of Europe consisting of experts from various member states, prepared a "draft European Convention for the Protection of Minorities", adopted by the Commission on 8 February, 1991 and submitted to the Committee of Ministers.[8]

In this draft the expression national minorities does not appear. In Article 2 there is also a definition of the concept of a minority: "a group which is smaller in number than the rest

[7] The Council of Europe, op. cit., p. 41

[8] *See generally*: Ibid., Chapter 5, pp. 36–39

of the population of a state whose members, although nationals of that state, have ethnic, religious or linguistic features different from those of the rest of the population, and are guided by the will to safeguard their culture, traditions, religion or language." (Article 2)

This definition, which could be applied also to national minorities and recognizes only a moderate degree of collective rights, seems to be more in favour of individual rights. The minority rights are in general for the benefit of persons/individuals belonging to minorities, but minorities as such are the beneficiaries of a lifestyle and identity, of protection against assimilationist policies and boundary manipulation and they enjoy effective participation (Article 9).

Eliminating the term national minority which has always been present in the Documents of the Council of Europe, the Commission prefers to deal with a more accepted individual rights policy among the members of the Commission. I think that the search for a consensus within the Commission and the will to find a solution explains both the elimination of the term national minorities and the reluctance to grant collective rights.

The project undoubtedly merits high attention because it attempts to reconcile the protection of minorities with the preservation of territorial integrity, sovereignty and political independence of states, and also attempts to introduce machinery to guarantee the rights of minorities.

This project is very often quoted as a working document for preparing other issues of the Council of Europe on minority rights.

The Austrian Draft Protocol

This document is important because "the scope is potentially wider than analogous texts on minorities in that the draft applies to "ethnic groups": other texts prepared within the ambit of the Council of Europe habitually refer to national minorities.[9]

For the first time in the context of a Council of Europe document the terms minority and national minority are not included.

The definition of the concept of ethnic groups recalls the definition of minority as: "a group of citizens within a state who *a)* are traditionally residents in the territory of a state; *b)* are smaller in number than the rest of the population of a state or a region within this state; *c)* have ethnical or linguistic features different from those of the rest of the population; *d)* have their own cultural identity" (Paragraph 1). In Article 3 it is stated that all rights in the Protocol may be enjoyed individually or in common with other members of their group. As a collective right the concession is granted to a group to choose deputies to represent it in public bodies (Paragraph 3).

The term minority was avoided but the concept remains the same. The Austrian Protocol underlines the idea that avoiding terms like national minorities and ethnic minorities could better promote the political acknowledgement of the protection of minority rights.

European Charter for Regional and Minority Languages (5 November, 1992)

The aim of this Charter is solely cultural. It wants to safeguard, develop and promote the regional or minority languages. It is not merely a principle of prohibiting negative discrimination but is based on the principle of equality: these languages can be used in social (school, media) and administrative (economic and judiciary) life.

[9] *See generally*: Ibid., pp. 26–27

The Charter is not *per se* an instrument on minority rights, but it clearly works for the benefit of speakers of minority languages. With this perspective the Charter is an acknowledgement of a collective right, namely a language. The concept of equality marks a big step forward in the acknowledgement of other collective rights. Unfortunately, many countries with large minority groups still remain outside this convention.[10]

Recommendation 1177 "on the Rights of Minorities" (1992)

Recommendation 1177 contributed to clarifying the concept of collective rights of national minorities. Articles 1 and 2 state that "History has transformed the continent of Europe into a mosaic of peoples... the mixing and overlapping of these peoples is such that it is impossible to define their geographical boundaries fully and exclusively. The national frontiers which emerged from two world wars did not achieve this. Nor will those of the future, whatever form they take." Article 3 underlines the fact that "In a democratic state there can be no second-class citizens: citizenship is the same for all".

The pragmatic approach of this statement achieved the aim of giving a concrete indication for helping governments to overcome the difficulties for promoting these rights within their own states.

The same Recommendation while noting that there is now a very large number of declarations of principles... advocating the recognition of minorities... claims an urgent need for international decisions and commitments which can be rapidly implemented in the area concerned (Articles 6 and 8).

[10] *See generally*: Ibid., Chapter 4, pp. 31–35

What Minorities?—What Rights?
Opinion of the Political Affairs Committee (Document 6749)

The Rapporteur of the Opinion of the Political Affairs Committee[11] explains very clearly the purpose of a specific definition of national minorities. It is said that because there are minorities of all kinds, drafting a Protocol should always keep in perspective the kind of minorities concerned. Not all minorities are national, and nowadays there are minorities who are facing different kinds of problems. An example of this is that "Hungarians in Romania are a national minority and their problems are comparable to those of the Turks in Bulgaria. Yet neither of these groups have any similarity with the Hindu minority in the United Kingdom or the Islamic minority in Europe... Muslims and Gypsies are quite clearly minorities in many countries of Europe, but they are not national minorities".

The conclusion is that a definition of national minority is very important to avoid a confusing approach to the problems of minorities, and the above explanation of the concept gives a better understanding of the identity of national minorities.

Recommendation 1201 (1 February, 1993) (The Draft Additional Protocol)

"In Recommendation 1201 (1993),[12] the Parliamentary Assembly of the Council of Europe recommended that the Committee of Ministers adopt an Additional Protocol to the European Convention on Human Rights drawing on the text

[11] Doc. 6749, prov. 26 January, 1993

[12] The draft is attached to Recommendation 1201 (1993) and refers to: *National Minorities and Their Members*.

of an Additional Protocol included in the Recommendation.[13] The draft Protocol is styled as one "Concerning the Rights of Persons belonging to National Minorities". The rights are defined as individual rights exercised, where appropriate, collectively (Paragraph 4).

"Defining them as collective rights would have entailed insurmountable problems for the recognition of 'national minorities', such as persons having legal personality... The choice of a protocol...implied the need to settle...the old argument over the individual as opposed to collective rights of national minorities."[14]

The definition of national minority refers to a group of persons in a state who: *a)* are citizens; *b)* maintain long-standing ties with the state; *c)* display distinctive ethnic, cultural, religious or linguistic characteristics; *d)* are sufficiently representative, although smaller in number than the rest of the population of that state; *e)* are motivated to preserve their common identity (traditions, religion, language) (Article 1a–e).

It is important to note that whereas the Austrian draft protocol uses the term "ethnic group", the Assembly draft prefers national minorities. The Assembly is more concerned with clarifying the identity of those to whom the rights are applied. The difference between ethnic groups and national minorities is essential on the grounds of the concrete application of these rights.

The Summit of Heads of State and Government of Member States (Vienna, October 1993)

The Council of Europe tried to introduce machinery to guarantee the rights of minorities. The Summit of the Heads of

[13] The Council of Europe, op. cit., p. 27

[14] Doc. 6742, 19 January, 1993, p. 4

State and Government of the Member States in Vienna (8–9 October, 1993) decided "to enter into political and legal commitments relating to the protection of national minorities in Europe, and to instruct the Committee of Ministers to elaborate appropriated international legal instruments".[15] The Committee of Ministers instructed an *ad hoc* committee for the protection of national minorities (CAHMIN) to draft, before June 1994, a "background convention" and to begin the drafting work of a Protocol no later than 31 December, 1994.[16]

Regarding concrete actions, the Council of Europe has launched numerous pilot projects in the form of cultural manifestations, aimed at confidence building between communities and minorities.

The CAHMIN Report and the Convention for the Protection of National Minorities

The "Framework Convention for the Protection of National Minorities" prepared by the CAHMIN was adopted on 10 November, 1994 (and the Framework Convention will be open for signature on the occasion of the first part of the 1995 Session of the Parliamentary Assembly—beginning of February 1995).

In the Interim Activity Report (Doc. 7109—21 June, 1994) it is stated that "As to the question of the definition of the notion of national minorities, the Committee has noted that such a definition was not needed for drawing up a draft Protocol to the ECHR since this Protocol would contain individual and

[15] The Vienna Summit Document. *See generally*: The Council of Europe, op. cit., pp. 3–4 and 14–15

[16] Doc. 7109, 21 June, 1994. Interim Activity Report I. Terms of reference of CAHMIN, nn. 1–2

universal rights... The Committee has agreed to adopt a pragmatic approach, i.e. to start the preparatory work without embarking on a prior discussion on the definition. It intends to pursue its work along this approach."[17]

The Committee relinquished the attempted commitment to giving a definition because as yet no definition acceptable to all the member states has been devised. The different approaches, of thc member states to the question of national minorities makes it impossible to find a generally accepted definition of national minority.

The Committee agreed to include stipulations defining certain objectives which the state parties would undertake to pursue. Such provisions are not self-operative, the state parties, concerning the implementation of objectives, can take their own particular circumstances into account.[18]

The Preamble indicates the aim of the Framework Convention: "The effective protection of national minorities and of the rights and the freedoms of persons belonging to those minorities, within the rule of law, respecting the territorial integrity and national sovereignty of states." It is also stated that "the upheavals of European history have shown that the protection of national minorities is essential to stability, democratic security and peace in this continent".

References are made to the commitments concerning the protection of national minorities in the U.N. and CSCE, particularly the Copenhagen Document of 29 June, 1990.

My opinion is that the Framework is the result of a difficult compromise. In a way it re-iterates that those rights should be understood on the one hand as individual rights (the Framework Convention repeats the familiar expression of "person belonging to a national minority") (Article 3), and on the other hand it is clear that their identity should be pro-

[17] Ibid., Paragraph 7

[18] Ibid., Paragraph 9

tected against any form of assimilation (Article 5). The identity is specified as always with the three characteristics of religion, language, traditions and cultural heritage (ethnicity) (Article 5).

I would conclude by noting that, though not manifestly stated, there is an underlying definition of the concept of national minorities in line with Recommendation 1201 (1993). This Framework Convention also remains faithful to the specific meaning of a national minority and to the distinction between national minority and ethnic minority.

Conclusions

Since its foundation in 1949, the "work" of the Council of Europe on national minorities had a pragmatic touch. Most documents are focused on standard-setting in the legal field. Recognizing the basic complexities of the concept of minority from the outset, the term national minority has been constantly retained so as to avoid the assimilation of these specific minorities with the majority of the dominant population and confusion with other minority groups. All categories of minorities, who are not national and are based on other criteria, for example migrant workers, political minorities, economic or social minorities, sexual minorities, are therefore excluded from the texts of the official Recommendations and Documents of the Council of Europe.

"The broad nature of the work of the Council of Europe means that it has undertaken a dedicated and concerted response to the minority question, implicating its structures for action and utilizing its considerable experience in the promotion of democracy, human rights and the rule of law."[19]

[19] The Council of Europe, op. cit., p. 14

I willingly quote the Vienna Declaration (Summit, October 1993), where it is stated that "Having regard to its fundamental vocation, the Council of Europe is particularly well placed *to contribute to the settlement* of problems of national minorities".

All efforts within the framework of the Council of Europe to achieve a definition of national minorities have failed due to a well-known political reluctance.

The co-operation started after the events of the 1990s, between the Council of Europe and the other international organizations (in particular the CSCE) is the path of achieving, even in this particular question, the best possible result.

In the international practice, minority rights are the rights of individuals, but the rights of peoples are collective rights. "The evolution of the Council of Europe is towards the increasing recognition of the visibility of minorities as subject rights...and it is appropriate that the Council of Europe should take a central role in moving from new perceptions to codes of legal and community practice."[20]

[20] Ibid., p. 19

CHAPTER VI

Towards a Definition of the Concept of National Minority

Interaction of the Documents of the U.N., CSCE and the Council of Europe

The analysis of the documents of the U.N., CSCE and the Council of Europe leads with different arguments to the same result: they have not succeeded in formulating a generally accepted definition of the concept of national minorities. Sadly, the definitions of the concepts of ethnic minorities and national minorities have been a subject of frequent, and I would say, almost obsessive concern of the various international organizations with no satisfactory conclusion.

Looking at the latest documents of the international organizations, it seems illusory to think that a positive solution will shortly be reached.

To summarize the experience of the U.N., CSCE and the Council of Europe it would seem that the difficulty in reaching a satisfactory definition acceptable to all, lies in the meaning ascribed to the term minority and to those referred to as minority groups.

The three international organizations agree on the fact that, while not considering the strong political reservations for achieving a definition, the World, and Europe in particular, knows an extreme variety of minority groups. Groups who are settled in well-defined settlement areas, groups dispersed throughout the whole or most of a state, groups divided between states, and nomadic groups. It is not possible to find an all-embracing definition of minorities. Therefore the practice of the three international organizations has been to try and identify *the minorities by means of objective indices* (language, ethnic group, religion, culture, number less than half of the population of the state, non-dominant position, citizenship) *and subjective indices* (will to preserve their culture, traditions, religion, language. Academically, the collective will to survive as a group). The meaning of the terms ethnic minority and national minority in the documents quoted in previous chapters incorporates the idea that minorities must also be citizens/nationals of the state in question. "This restriction of the citizenship is not clear if it results from the words national or minority or the two in combination: some definitions of minority alone (unaccompanied by national) incorporate the same restriction". A definitive view is not yet present in general international law.[1]

According to the three international organizations the minority status should be granted on the basis of the objective and subjective indices of any group claiming it.

All other categories founded on other criteria: foreign residents, immigrants, foreign workers, economic minorities, sexual minorities, oppressed majorities, dominant minorities, are therefore excluded from the scope of all the texts of the three international organizations.

The basis of the objective and subjective elements doubtless helps to restrict the status of minority to a certain kind of group, but does not eliminate the confusion which arises also in those groups which are recognized in their objective and subjective elements.

In the three international organizations the terms minority and national minority are used as synonyms, because no well-defined distinction between ethnic and national minorities exists. In the *traveaux preparatoires* preceding the draft of the documents of the three international organizations, we some-

[1] See: The Council of Europe, op. cit., pp. 12–13

times find that the word national refers to the historical circumstances peculiar to them, those circumstances established their existence as national minorities.[2]

Another common denominator in the three international organizations is the discussion on individual and collective minority rights. Even if different emphasis is placed on the two kinds of rights, I would say that there is a general consensus on the fact that minority rights are proposed as instruments of group protection and the collective practice is vital. There are individual rights with a collective dimension, not strictly collective rights.[3] The rights of groups are collective rights, but international legal practice underlines the fact that rights are granted to persons belonging to the groups.

The analysis of these documents shows how important it is to achieve a definition of national minority. This definition would finally clarify, theoretically or academically, the term minority (referred to as the ethnic minority) and national minority (referred to as the historical circumstances peculiar to some groups). I have already indicated the incongruity of using these two terms as if they were synonymous, and the documents in fact assimilate the two different kinds of minorities under the same concept, without considering that a clarification of the terms would place a new emphasis on the whole question of minorities in the acknowledgement of the specific rights belonging to both minority groups.

A definition of the concept of national minorities will be welcomed not only in the framework of expert research to resolve an academic deficiency, but would lead also to a better settlement of the minorities' demands and expectations in the areas concerned.

[2] *See generally*: AS/Jur, op. cit., p. 13
[3] The Council of Europe, op. cit., p. 17

The pessimism of the international organizations about achieving a satisfactory definition of national minorities could be overcome only with closer co-operation among them. Unfortunately, at present, the co-operation (especially between the U.N. and the Council of Europe and CSCE) mainly takes place through reciprocal invitations to participate in meetings of the Secretariat. However, after the events of 1990, I should not minimize the worthwhile co-operation between the CSCE and the Council of Europe, which has become, I would say, more closer this year on the occasion of the preparation of the Framework Convention for the Protection of National Minorities. Even if the existence of established structures for co-operation in this field is remote, the path of co-operation could indeed abolish pessimism and remove political reluctance.

Doctrinal Opinions

I consider it interesting to proceed from the international organizations' statements on the doctrine. It is very important to examine what the doctrine has said on the concept of a minority. I shall quote seven authors, who have tried to resolve the problem of the definition of a minority.

Mr. De Azcárate

For 12 years, Mr. De Azcárate was head of the section on the minority questions, at the time of the League of Nations and the minority treaties. "My personal experience... leads me to the conclusion that... a national minority is the existence of a national consciousness, accompanied by linguistic and cultural differences."[4] The author speaking of national minorities declares: "In general terms, the expression national minority refers to a more or less considerable proportion of the citizens of a state who are of a different nationality from that of the majority".

Mr. De Azcárate, while retaining language and culture, tended to eliminate religion as a distinctive criterion of a minority. He stressed that freedom of conscience and of religion in modern states, makes the specific guarantee of a minority's religious rights superfluous.

In Mr. De Azcárate's definition the most distinguished criterion of a minority is the "existence of a national consciousness".

Mr. T. Modeen

This author excludes non-citizens from a concept of minority, and he retains the criterion of a numerically smaller group: "There are no typical national minorities, only a number of different groups which may be described as such."[5]

This opinion refers only to one aspect of the definition of a minority and does not clarify identity.

Seminar Held in Ohrid—Yugoslavia (1974)

One of the participants proposed the following definition of the term minority: "A group of citizens, sufficient in number to pursue the aims of the group, but numerically smaller than

[4] Proposal concerning a definition of the term "minority" submitted by Mr. J. Deschênes. Doc. E/CN.4/Sub. 2/1985/31, 14 May, 1985, p. 24. *See generally*: De Azcárate, P., *League of Nations and National Minorities: An Experiment*. Washington 1945

[5] Ibid., p. 25; *See generally*: Modeen, T., *The International Protection of National Minorities in Europe*, Abo 1969

the rest of the people, linked together by historical, ethnic, cultural and religious or linguistic ties and wishing to preserve such ties, which are different from those of the rest of the people."[6]

This definiton is based on the acknowledgement of some objective criteria, but does not make any reference to the non-dominant position of a minority.

Ms B. Elles

For this author the distinction between ethnic minorities and national minorities is of relevant importance. National minority refers to "persons who belong to a group owing allegiance on account of nationality to a state other than the one in which they are residing and who are numerically less than the other inhabitants of the state of residence".[7] This definition underlines the specific identity of a national minority but does not include citizenship. So the term national minority could be also referred to resident aliens.

Mr. F. Capotorti

Capotorti made strenuous efforts to improve the definition of the concept of minorities. The result of his work is the following: A minority "is a group numerically inferior to the rest of the population of a state in a non-dominant position, whose members—being nationals of the state—possess ethnic, religious or linguistic characteristics differing from those of the rest of the population and show, if only implicitly, a sense of

[6] Ibid., p. 25
[7] Ibid., pp. 15–16.

solidarity, directed towards preserving their culture, traditions, religion or language."[8]

This definition is one of the most complete and has been discussed by governments. Contemporary studies of the concept of national minorities always refer to this definition. I also find this definition very close to my objective in this book, though the meaning of the term national minorities in this context remains to be clarified.

I refer to some Government comments to this definition:

The Permanent Representative of France to the U.N. noted, in 1976, that in reference to Capotorti's study, the French Government, under the terms of the Constitution of the French Republic, does not agree with the very principle of such a study. The French people recognized no distinction based on ethnic characteristics and thus ruled out any concept of minority.[9]

Finland pointed out that: "Thc expression 'nationals of the state' used by Capotorti in his definition is somewhat vague, since in a state there may exist several different nationalities as presupposed in the UNESCO Convention Against Discrimination in Education. A more accurate expression would be 'citizens of the state' ".

The Canadian Government suggested that in Mr. Capotorti's definition the words "inferior to" and "rest" should be replaced respectively by "smaller than the sum of" and "others."[10]

[8] Doc. E/CN.4/Sub. 2/1977/385, rev. 1, p. 102. *See generally*: Capotorti, F., I diritti dei membri delle minoranze: verso una dichiarazione delle Nazioni Unite? in: *Rivista di Diritto Internazionale* LXVI (1981), pp. 30–42

[9] Proposal concerning, op. cit., p. 27

[10] Ibid., p. 28

Mr. A. Eide

A definition was offered by the U.N. Rapporteur, Eide: "A minority is any group of persons resident within a sovereign state which constitutes less than half of the population of the national society and whose members share common characteristics of an ethnic, religious or linguistic nature that distinguish them from the rest of the population."[11]

This definition is vague and does not distinguish between citizens and non-citizens, traditional group and immigrants, "old" and "new" arrivals. It seems more of a working definition than a scientific resolution. It is difficult to see the practical use of this definition.

Mr. J. Deschênes

With this opinion, submitted to the U.N. Sub-Commission on Prevention of Discrimination and Protection of Minorities, Mr. Deschênes gives a definition of minority "in the light of the Ohrid Seminar and the work done by Mr. Capotorti".[12] He includes the following elements: distinguishable groups; ethnic, religious or linguistic characteristics; number less than half of the population of the state; non-dominant situation; citizenship; solidarity; collective will to survive. Consequently, he proposed the following definition: "A group of citizens of a state, constituting a numerical minority and in a non dominant position in that state, endowed with ethnic, religious or linguistic characteristics which differ from those of the majority of the population, having a sense of solidarity with one another, motivated, if only implicitly, by a collective will

[11] U.N. Doc. E/CN.4/Sub. 2/1993/34, Paragraph 29

[12] Proposal concerning, op. cit., p. 30

to survive and whose aim is to achieve equality with the majority in fact of law."[13]

This definition collects elements of both the Ohrid Seminar and Mr. Capotorti's concepts, adding a more precise idea of how to achieve the aim of a minority, which is to preserve its identity. Deschênes' definition adds the collective will to survive and the equality with a majority in fact and in law.

This definition would seem quite satisfactory, but still does not distinguish between a national minority and an ethnic minority. The definition recognizes equal status for both minority groups. My conclusion is that this definition could be generally accepted on the meaning of a minority, but does not include the historical background of national minorities. I think that currently the term national minority requires the support of conceptual clarification.

The doctrine on the concept of a minority gave a clear understanding of the criteria which should be applied for formulating a generally acceptable definition of this concept. Some of the above-quoted criteria (citizenship, non-dominant position, will to survive as a group, ethnic, linguistic and religious characteristics) have already been introduced into the documents of the international organizations on minorities, others are still not well accepted by numerous states (the meaning of the term nationals as an element of identity, the sense of solidarity, the national consciousness, the historical reference of the term national).

The doctrine, however, provides enlightenment to the politician, who also has the duty to take these theoretical concepts and insert them into the specific documents.

[13] Ibid., p. 30

State and Government Observations and Acceptances

Bilateral Agreements

The definitions of ethnic minority and national minority became highly relevant also to states and governments who want to approve by legislation the rights of minorities living within their own territories. Bilateral agreements between two states having the same minority group within their own territories, or states having persons belonging to their own ethnic group living as a minority in the territory of other states, is becoming common practice now in Europe.

Examples of these bilateral agreements are those between Hungary and Slovenia, Italy and Slovenia, Poland and Lithuania, Hungary and Ukraine, Germany and Poland.

Even if these agreements are different both in content and form, there are four common features:

a) Conjoint declarations, a kind of "soft-law", avoiding strict interpretations which could also be required by minority groups not expressly mentioned in the declaration.

b) Rights of minority groups as rights of human persons, and not as group rights.

c) Menu-list of rights, which are those mentioned in the international organizations' documents.

d) Reciprocity in fulfilling the obligations of the declaration.[14]

The concept of national minority underlined in those bilateral agreements is a pragmatic one and refers to a group of citizens smaller than the rest of the population of a state

[14] *See*: Buonomo, V., op. cit., pp. 13–14

linked by an identity that has ethnic and cultural, linguistic and religious characteristics, who want to preserve such an identity even through cross-border contact with their compatriots.

In fact, the examples of the agreements quoted above deal with a particular group of minorities, who are national minorities. Those national minorities have arisen with the redefining of frontiers after the two wars. I would reflect on the fact that it seems clear that states with national minorities in their territories make a distinction between them and other ethnic minorities. This distinction includes the specific right of cross-border contact (only for keeping their own identity, excluding the right of so-called "external" self-determination or secessionism) with their own country.

In the documents of the international organizations and even in the doctrine, the concept of national minorities was generally assimilated to other ethnic minorities. Also the Pope's Message for the World Day of Peace (1 January, 1989): "To build peace respect minorities", refers to minorities as communities with their own backgrounds of cultural, ethnic, linguistic and religious traditions and history.[15]

The awakening of the nationalistic movements in Europe obliged states and, I would say also, the international organizations to reflect on the expression national minorities as a concept distinct from ethnic minorities. The proof of this new concept is the fact that the expression national minorities is currently more in use in international organizations' documents, since 1990.[16]

[15] Il Messaggio per la Giornata Mondiale della Pace 1989: Per costruire la Pace rispettare le Minoranze, Giovedì 8 Dicembre 1988. in: *Insegnamenti di Giovanni Paolo* II–XI, 4, Citta del Vaticano, pp. 1788–1797 (Paragraph 2)

[16] *See*: Buonomo, V., op. cit., p. 15

Examples of Official Documents of Some Central and Eastern European Countries on Minorities

Several countries included in their constitutions or laws the rights of minorities. I selected only three examples of Central and Eastern European countries to give an idea of the efforts of governments to adopt concrete measures for protecting minority rights.

The Hungarian Law

Among the first specific laws on the rights of national and ethnic minorities approved after the fall of communism in Central and Eastern Europe is Act LXXVII passed by the Hungarian National Assembly at its session of 7 July, 1993. As is known since 1919, Hungary is among the countries with the largest minority group living outside its borders. This law acknowledges "all those groups having been living on the territory of Hungary for at least one century, are to be regarded as national and ethnic minorities who constitute a numerical minority within the population of the country, whose members hold Hungarian citizenship, and who differ from the rest of the population in terms of their own language, cultures and traditions, *and who prove to be aware of the cohesion, national or ethnic*, which is to aim at preserving all these and at articulating and safeguarding the interests of their respective historically developed communities."(Chapter 1, Section 1.2)[17]

Section 2 states that "the present Act is not to be applied to refugees, immigrants, permanent resident aliens and to stateless persons".

This definition does not openly mention religion among the characteristics of a minority group, and stresses the elements

[17] The English version of the law can be seen in the *Bull. Nat. Ethn. Min. in Hungary*, 1, issued by the Office for National and Ethnic Minorities.

of cohesion, national or ethnic (this difference is important). The definition recalls the one formulated by Mr. De Azcárate. The criteria to identify a minority include: "mother tongue, cultures and traditions". Loyalty to "their respective historically developed communities" seems rather clear. I think that the period of a century refers to the particular historical background of Hungary, rather than to a discriminatory period for acknowledging of a minority group. The other objective elements of this definition are common to standard concepts in documents of the international organizations on minorities.

My opinion is that this law is a good law, and I do hope that it can be rapidly implemented.

The Romanian Constitution

The Constitution of Romania,[18] approved on 8 December, 1991, with a "referendum", contains dispositions and rights for protecting minority groups.

Article 4 of the General Principles clearly declares the protection of national minorities and guarantees them the right of keeping their ethnic, religious, linguistic and cultural identities.

The same Article explains that the identity of national minorities is understood as non-discriminatory and equal towards the other Romanian citizens.

It is interesting to note how the concept of identity of a minority group is emphasized. Romania is a country with large minority groups living within its borders, and the concept of identity is important in order to protect the ethnicity of each minority group. In this way the use of the terms ethnic and

[18] The Constitution of Romania. *See*: *La Cadre Législatif et Institutionnel pour les minorités nationales de Roumanie*. Institute Roumain pour le Droits de l'Homme, Bucharest 1994

national referred to the minorities is also welcomed in the Constitution.

The rights of minorities in the Constitution are listed according to the standards of international documents.

The Constitution does not contain a definition of a national minority, which probably will be included in the law on minorities currently under the Parliament's consideration.

The Albanian Law

The Albanian Law referred to minorities in its Charter of Rights and the concept of minorities is quite interesting because in Article 26 after listing the rights of minorities it states that "Nationality (of minorities) shall be determined on the basis of accepted international norms". This expression is new but at the same time vague. In fact, it would encourage the international arena to define the concept of nationality.[19]

Definition of a National Minority

According to what I have so far stated, the question of a definition of a national minority is more far-reaching than it appears at first. The international organizations after many years of effort have been forced to admit their failure to reach a generally well-accepted definition on minorities. However, after the events of 1989 and 1990, there are special factors which, for the first time, shed light on the path towards a definition. In 1989 within the area of "forced stability", that was Eastern Europe, there was a series of profound and decisive changes in political, economic and cultural life. These changes are a challenge to the stability of democracy and peace in Europe. The fact that the concept of a nation, which the

[19] Law No. 506, 31 March, 1993

Marxist–Leninist doctrine intended to obliterate in the name of proletarian internationalism, has once again become front-page news. While Western Europe appeared to have evolved a balanced situation, even if this is not fully accepted by the minorities themselves, as certain residual forms of violence indicate (Corsica, Basque country, South Tyrol), Central and Eastern Europe are facing violent demonstrations of nationalism, as evidenced by the current tragic situation in the former Yugoslavia.

Clearly, the use of the term national minority remains a source of difficulty, given the lack of a precise definition, for distinguishing it from other ethnic minorities. The assimilation of the concept of national minority into ethnic minority seems to be already accepted and included in the documents of the international organizations, and also the doctrine does not always consider national minorities as distinct minorities. I would say that in the past four decades it was not strictly necessary to distinguish the two minority concepts, and in fact most of the rights of ethnic minorities are also the rights of national minorities.

A response to the recent revival of the nationalist minority movements could be a clarification of the concept of national minorities. The specific characteristics of national minorities were quite clear at the end of the First World War, for this reason I consider that for a definition of national minorities a short lesson in history would be pertinent.

The Help of History

To understand the present map of Europe it is necessary to go back at least as far as 1919. "A pupil and a teacher in 1900 would certainly have been more adept than we are at dealing with the concept of nationality"[20] which has perplexed us over the past four years.

[20] Council of Europe. DECS/SE/BS/Sem. (91) 2, p. 21

The disappearance of the Iron Curtain has highlighted the fact that the map of Europe in the 20th century was drawn up twice as a result of the two World Wars.

The perceptible outbreaks of nationalist fervour in Central and Eastern Europe since 1989 are the direct outcome of the choice of frontiers made by the victors in 1918. *However, it would be naïve to compare 1918 and 1989.* But we cannot ignore the concepts and the solutions given to national minority problems after the First World War.

As I tried to demonstrate in Chapter I of this book, the term national minority refers to those minorities which had historical origins: they were separated from their fellow citizens by the creation of new states, but they maintained their identity and characteristics while forming part of a state which was not their country of origin. This applied, for example, to Hungarians and Turks living outside Turkey and Hungary.

The other type of minorities, whom I have called ethnic minorities are those groups with a clearly marked identity (cultural, linguistic, religious, etc.), who have been living for centuries in a part of state territory where they form genuine communities. The examples are well known: the Catalans, the Basques, the Scots, the Corsicans, etc.[21]

Can a Single Definition Cover the Concept of Minority in the Broad Sense of Ethnic and National Minorities?

I believe that the answer to this question could be positive if within a single definition a distinction were made between the concept of nationality (minorities with historical origins) and ethnicity (minorities with a marked identity living for centuries in a given state). This distinction is important because, among the rights granted to national minorities, free cultural

[21] Doc. 6749, op. cit., Paragraph 10

cross-border contacts with the country of origin should be included. But it should be very clear that these contacts do not touch the sovereignty of the states and violate their territorial integrity. Separatist movements should also not be encouraged.

If one could choose between the legal formula of individual rights and that of collective rights to protect minorities, there is no doubt that personally I would choose the collective rights, because where minorities are concerned some of these rights are, by definition, collective rights. But I am well aware that the documents of the international organizations generally refer only to individual rights. The only solution therefore is to grant rights to everyone who belongs to a national minority: "Individual rights with a collective dimension."[22]

What is a National Minority?

I am not the first to undertake the task of giving a definition, as probably I will not be the last; however, in light of what I have said in the previous sections I propose *the following definition of a national minority*:

"A group of citizens of a state, numerically inferior to the rest of the population of that state and in a non-dominant position, who because of historical events have been separated from their country of origin, maintaining the religious, linguistic and cultural characteristics of that country, having a collective will to survive and which aims at achieving equality with the majority in fact and in law, while respecting the sovereignty of the state."

This definition has some affinity to the concepts of Mr. Capotorti, the Ohrid Seminar and Mr. Deschênes, but it differs from those because of the specific insertion of the historical

[22] The Council of Europe, op. cit., p. 17

origin and links of national minorities with their motherland, together with the declaration of loyalty to the sovereignty of the adopted state.

I believe that the urgent need to find a constructive and peaceful solutions to the nationalist phenomena should also take cognizance of a clarification of the concept of a national minority. This could, on the one hand, lead to a better understanding of the expectations of the national minorities; and on the other induce governments and states to have a more tolerant approach towards those expectations.

What Kind of Multicultural Society is Needed?

At the beginning of this book I said that the concept of multicultural society is vague which also generates confusion. Very often terms like multicultural and multi-ethnic society are applied synonymously. The concept of ethnicity has more exclusive connotations than culture. Groups with a common culture simply share certain values and forms of behaviour (like students). Ethnicity is a characteristic which refers to "inherited" forms of belonging, and takes precedence over any other characteristics of a given group.

The concept of national minorities is linked to the process of a historical insertion of a national group into another nation-state. This insertion is not a free choice of the people involved, but it is the result of a political compromise achieved by treaties or agreements. Multi-ethnic pluralism cannot be assimilated to the multicultural pluralism introduced by immigrants, aliens, or refugees, etc., because the expectations of the latter are very different from the rights that should be granted to the ethnic and national minorities. I am thinking specifically of the so-called "internal self-determination" (linguistic and cultural and, in certain cases, administrative autonomy). Even if many immigrant groups are in a minority situation the documents of the international organizations never included immigrants or other kinds of minority groups among the ethnic and national minorities.

As a result of these conceptual clarifications, it is important *to avoid the following ambiguous concepts* in reference to a definition of a multicultural society:[23]

1. To describe society as a mosaic of organized communities where cultural, ethnic or religious groups simply exist side by side, would be a "static" conception of society, because there is interaction and communication between individuals and groups. It is not correct to suggest that people belonging to one group or another should be "confined" to their own life style without any communication

2. To understand society as a "melting pot" like in North America, where different cultures are fused in a conglomerate of cosmopolitan culture, should be avoided because each person should rctain his own ethnic identity, especially if there is a will to survive as an ethnic group.

3. To regard minorities in general (including the non-ethnic minorities) as a natural park where one can admire beautiful trees or plants without touching them, because they are in a reserved area, would in fact put minority groups under the political control of the state, and discourage the integration of such groups into social life.

The best definition of a multicultural society is a reality where "the communities to which people belong function as systems of social organizations, in solidarity and with autonomy that should be recognized".[24] But I fear that this concept could appear idealistic.

15 January, 1995

[23] *See generally*: Perotti, A., op. cit., pp. 9–19

[24] Council of Europe: Community and ethnic relations in Europe, MG-CR (91) 1, Final E, Paragraph 33

Bibliography

Sources

Chapter I. The concept of National Minorities at the End of the First World War

1. President Wilson's Speech at the Plenary Session of the Peace Conference, May 31st, 1919.
2. Resolutions of the Council of the League of Nations Concerning Minority Protection Guarantee Procedures:
   a) Report presented by M. Tittoni and adopted by the Council of the League of Nations on October 22nd, 1920.
   b) Resolutions adopted by the Council on October 25th, 1920.
   c) Resolution adopted by the Council on June 27th, 1921.
   d) Resolution adopted by the Council on September 5th, 1923.
   e) Resolution adopted by the Council on June 10th, 1925.
   f) Resolution adopted by the Council on June 13th, 1929.
3. Permanent Court of International Justice:
   a) Advisory Opinion on the Greco-Bulgarian Communities—Report B/7—1930.
   b) Advisory Opinion on Minority Schools in Albania—April 6th, 1935—Reports AB/64—1935.

Chapter II. The Concept of National Minority in the 1930s and Soon After World War II

1. The Charter of the United Nations (U.N., 1945).
2. Universal Declaration of Human Rights (U.N., 1948).
3. General Assembly Resolution 217C (III), entitled *Fate of Minorities* (U.N., 1948).
4. Convention on the Prevention and Punishment of the Crime of Genocide (U.N., 1948).
5. Study of the Legal Validity of the Undertakings Concerning Minorities. U.N. Doc. E/CN.4/1950/367.

Chapter III. The U.N. Concept of Minority

1. Convention Concerning Discrimination in Respect of Occupation (ILO, 1958).
2. International Convention on the Elimination of All Forms of Racial Discrimination (U.N., 1965).
3. International Covenant on Civil and Political Rights (U.N., 1966).
4. Declaration on the Elimination of All Forms of Intolerance and of Discrimination Based on Religion or Belief (U.N., 1981).
5. Declaration on the Rights of Persons Belonging to National or Ethnic, Religious and Linguistic Minorities (U.N., 1992).
6. General Comment Adopted by the Human Rights Committee under Article 40, Paragraph 4, of the International Covenant on Civil and Political Rights—ADDENDUM—CCPR/C/21/Rev.1/Add.5/1994.
7. Commission of Human Rights—Sub-Commission on Prevention of Discrimination and Protection of Minorities. U.N. Doc.E/CN.4/Sub.2/1977/385.
8. Commission of Human Rights—Sub-Commission on Prevention of Discrimination and Protection of Minorities. U.N. Doc.E/CN.4/Sub.2/1985/31.
9. Commission of Human Rights—Sub-Commission on Prevention of Discrimination and Protection of Minorities. U.N. Doc. E/CN.4/Sub.2/1993/34.

Chapter IV. The Concept of Minority in the CSCE Process

1. Final Act of Helsinki (CSCE, 1975).
2. Concluding Document of the Follow-up Meeting of Vienna (CSCE, 1989).
3. The Document of the Second Meeting of the Conference on the Human Dimension of the CSCE, Copenhagen (1990).
4. Charter of Paris for a New Europe (CSCE, 1990).
5. Report of the CSCE Meeting of Experts on National Minorities (Geneva 1991).
6. The Document of the Third Meeting of the Conference on the Human Dimension of the CSCE, Moscow (1991).
7. The Helsinki Document 1992: The Challenges of Change (1992). 1st Helsinki Summit Declaration. IInd Helsinki Decision.
8. Reports of the Moderators at the Human Dimension Seminar on National Minorities, Warsaw (1993).

Chapter V. The Concept of Minority in the Context of the Council of Europe

1. The European Convention on the Human Rights and Fundamental Freedoms (Council of Europe 1950).
2. Council of Europe:
   Recommendation 285 (1961).
   Recommendation 814 (1977).
   Recommendation 1134 (1990).

Recommendation 1177 (1992).
Recommendation 1201 (1993).
3. The European Commission for Democracy Through Law (Venice Commission). *Draft European Convention for the Protection of Minorities* (8 February, 1991).
4. Council of Europe. *The European Charter for Regional and Minority Language* (5 November, 1992).
5. Council of Europe: *Framework Convention for the Protection of National Minorities*. Prepared by the CAHMIN (10 November, 1994).

Chapter VI. Towards a Definition of the Concept of National Minority

1. U.N.—Commission on Human Rights—Sub-Commission on Prevention of Discrimination and Protection of Minorities. Proposal concerning a definition of the term minority. Rapporteur, Mr. J. Deschênes. E/CN.4/Sub.2/1985/31.
2. U.N.—Commission on Human Rights—Sub-Commission on Prevention of Discrimination and Protection of Minorities. Report on constructive national arrangements for minorities. Rapporteur, A. Eide. E/CN.4/Sub.2/1993/34.
3. The Constitution of Romania (8 December, 1991).
4. Republic of Albania *Charter of Rights* Law No. 506-31, March 1993.
5. Act LXXVII of 1993 *On the Rights of National and Ethnic Minorities* (Hungarian National Assembly, 7 July, 1993).

Studies

Compilation of Documents

Wallenberg Raoul Institute of Human Rights and Humanitarian Law, Report No. 17: *A Compilation of Minority Rights Standard* (printed in Sweden 1993).

The Conference on Security and Co-operation in Europe, Analysis and Basic Documents 1972–1993. Ed. by A. Bloed, Dordrecht 1993.

The Council of Europe and Minorities—CoEMIN—September 1994.

Books and Articles

Alfredsson, G., Turk, D., International Mechanism for the Monitoring and Protection of Minorities Rights: Their Advantages, Disadvantages and Interrelationships, in: *Monitoring Human Rights in Europe*. Ed. by A. Bloca, Dordrecht 1992, pp. 169–186.

Alfredsson, G., De Zayas, A., Minority Rights: Protection by the United Nations, in: *Human Rights Law Journal*, 1–2 (1993).

Andrysek, O., Report on the Definition of Minorities. Institute of Human Rights, The Netherlands. SIM special No. 8, Utrecht 1989.

Bokatola, I. O., *L'Organisation des Nations Unies et la protection dés minorités*. Bruxelles 1992.

Bruum, G., Mamatey, S., *The World in the Twentieth Century*. Boston 1962.

Buonomo, V., *Riflessioni in tema di tutela delle minoranze alla luce di recenti sviluppi del Diritto Internazionale, Roma* (in press) 1994.

Capotorti, F., I diritti dei membri di minoranze: verso una dichiarazione delle Nazioni Unite? in: *Rivista di Diritto Internazionale* LXVI (1981), 30–42.

Capotorti, F., Il regime delle minoranze nel sistema delle Nazioni Unite e secondo l'art. 27 del patto sui diritti civili e politici, in: *Rivista di Diritto Internazionale dei Diritti dell'Uomo* V (1992), 102–112.

Carrascosa Coso, A., *La Santa Sede y la Conferencia sobre la Seguridad y la Cooperación en Europa*, Cuenca 1990.

Chabot, F., *L'idea di Nazione*. Bari 1961.

Chevalier, J. J., *Le grandi opere del pensiero politico*. Bologna, 1968.

De Azcárate, P., *League of Nations and National Minorities: An Experiment*. Washington 1945.

Ermarcora, F., The Protection of Minorities Before the United Nations, in: *Recueil des Cours*, 182 (1983) 250–257.

Feinberg, N., *La question des minorités à la Conférence de la paix de 1919–1920 e l'action juive en faveur de la protection internationale des minorités*. Paris 1929.

Galantai, J., *Trianon and the Protection of Minorities*. Budapest, 1992.

Ghebali, V. Y., *La Diplomatie de la Détente: La CSCE, 1973–1989*. Bruxelles 1989.

Hannum, H., *Autonomy Sovereignty and Self-Determination*. Philadelphia 1990.

Huber, K. J., Zaagman R., Towards the Prevention of Ethnic Conflict in CSCE: The High Commissioner on National Minorities and Other Developments. *International Journal of Group Rights*, 1 (1993), 51–58.

Lannung, M., The Rights of Minorities in: *Melanges Offerts a Polys Modinos*. Paris 1968.

Lemer, N., *Group Rights and Discrimination in International Law*. Dordrecht 1993.

Lloyd, D. G., *The Truth about the Peace Treaties*. London 1938.

Macartney, C. A., *National States and National Minorities*. London 1934.

Modeen, T., *The International Protection of National Minorities in Europe*. Abo 1969.

Nazionalismo e Cristianesimo. in: *La Civiltà Cattolica*, 3391, 5 ottobre 1991, 3–14.

Nesi, G., Soluzione pacifica delle controversie in Europa: recenti sviluppi nella CSCE. in: *La Comunità Internazionale*, XLVIII/2 (1993), 235–277.

Perotti, A., Pluralismo culturale e minoranze—Ambiguità da evitare. in: *People on the Move* XXII, March 1993, 3–19.

Rosas, A., Allan C., Helgesen, J., *The Strength of Diversity: Human Rights and Pluralist Democracy*. Dordrecht 1991.

Stone, J., *International Guarantees of Minority Rights*. Oxford–London 1932.

Temperley, H.W.V., *A History of the Peace Conference of Paris*. London 1924.

The Nationalities Question—from Versailles to the Present Day. European Teachers' Seminar, Esneux, Belgium, April 1991, Council of Europe DECS/SE/BS/Sem. (91).

Thornberry, P., *International Law and the Rights of Minorities.* Oxford 1992.

Winkler, W., *Statistiches Handbuch der europäischen Nationalitäten.* Berlin 1931.

Wolfrum, R., The Emergence of "New Minorities" as a Result of Migration. in: Brolmann, C., Lefeber, R. and Zieck, M. (eds): *People and Minorities in International Law.* Dordrecht 1993, pp. 153–166.